C000229080

SIMPLE
SURVIVAL

Copyright © 2019

Simple Survival:
The Ultimate Guide to Preparing for
Dangerous Situations and Emergency Survival

Justin W. Meyer

IMMUTABLE
PUBLISHING

All rights reserved. No part of this publication may be reproduced, distributed, or transmitted in any form or by any means, including photocopying, record-ing, or electronic or mechanical methods, without prior written permission of the publisher, except in the case of brief quotations embodied in reviews and certain other non-commercial uses permitted by copyright law.

Neither the author nor the publishers can accept any responsibility for any loss, injury or damage caused as a result of the techniques described in this publi-cation, nor for any prosecutions or proceedings brought or instigated against any person or body that may result from using these techniques. The first aid procedures described in this publication are not intended to be a substitute for professional medical care. The author and publisher expressly recommend the use of proper safety procedures when implementing techniques within this publication. Misuse of this information could result in serious injury for which the author and publisher disclaim liability.

ISBN: 978-1-7329415-0-2 (pbck), 978-1-7329415-1-9 (epub)

Editor: Qat Wanders, Wandering Words Media
Interior Layout and Design: MartinPublishingServices.com
Artwork: Bill Wittmann and Līna Stiprā
Cover Design: haley_graphics2

SIMPLE SURVIVAL

The Ultimate Guide to Preparing for Dangerous Situations and Emergency Survival

J. W. MEYER

IMMUTABLE PUBLISHING

FOR MOM

Your teaching, guidance and love has woven itself into immeasurable aspects of my life.

I am a better man because of it!

CONTENTS

INTRODUCTION

The world that we live in is unpredictable. It's full of hazards that can develop in a moment's notice. I don't mean to paint a grim picture, but catastrophic weather, shocking accidents, and terrifying acts are part of our reality. Don't believe me? Just turn on the world news for a week! One day is likely enough.

This guide will provide you with valuable knowledge that will allow you to properly confront these situations when they arise. My book lays out simple guidance and procedures that can be used by people of all backgrounds and skill levels—young and old alike.

Since childhood, I have studied and implemented survival techniques into my life by trial and error. Throughout my adult life, I have been involved with a group of close friends who have taken any survival information we could find and actually tested it in the field. I have also spent time in the military serving as a U.S. Army Airborne Ranger. As a soldier, fighting in multiple combat deployments, I learned a great deal concerning this topic. My years of experience have taken me into every one of earth's climate zones (except the arctic), but as a long-time resident of Wisconsin, I am no stranger to the extreme cold either. That being said, you do not need a list of credentials or years of practice to benefit from this book.

By incorporating these tips and basic skills you will become mentally stronger, more resourceful, and better prepared for potentially hazardous situations. Before long, you will find that much of what you learn here is going to find its way into your everyday life and it will come through paths that you never expected. Get used to saying, I'm glad I was ready for that!

Often, we are not talking about life and death here. There is a good chance that you will frequently use these skills to help others who were not prepared. I am not a doctor, but there have been a great many times that a bit of knowledge and some common medical supplies have come into play.

Once, two of my survival companions and I were on a two-week canoe trip into a remote wilderness area in Northern Minnesota and Canada called the Boundary Waters. It is a place of profound beauty that is virtually untouched by civilization. While at camp one afternoon, another canoe came over to us in need of help. One of the guys in their group had seriously cut his hand while preparing food and they could not get the bleeding to stop. The simple med kit they brought only had a few small bandages.

They were not prepared. I was able to provide them with some crucial knowledge and coagulation powder to stop the bleeding. With heavy bandage and gauze, he was able to properly wrap the wound. Would that guy have died? I am quite certain that he would have made it, but they were a few days from civilization and that is a long time to bleed! The point is that with a bit of know-how and the right supplies, I was able to help make a difference.

I can honestly guarantee that the things you learn in this book will allow you to make a difference too. There is a profound satisfaction that comes with being able to help another. That canoer was someone that I didn't know and will never see again. Think about your friends and family. How deeply do you care about them? I promise that one day when you least expect it, you WILL need this information.

Don't be the one who says it won't happen to me. It's a trap for the weak! Don't be the one who is afraid and helpless when things get ugly or you and your loved ones are in need. The regret will leave you numb with emptiness. Be the one who others look to because you have the solution. Be the one who has what is needed when the time comes. Be the one who will confidently take action that is reinforced with the proper knowledge. You CAN be the one who is able to make the difference!

Through countless experiences, this knowledge has proven itself time and time again. Some of this wisdom, simple though it may be, has remained valid for thousands of years. Other portions will incorporate the use of modern advancements. Each chapter of Simple Survival will bring you closer to being prepared for the worst. The pieces are here. Now, it's time to pick up what you've been missing.

WHY SURVIVAL?

"Hunger, love, pain, fear are some of those inner
forces which rule the individual's instinct for
self-preservation."

—Albert Einstein

Survival skills are for everyone. It is something that has followed humanity since the dawn of time. Unfortunately, as
years passed, the ease of modern convenience and technology has
taken us farther and farther away from those critical skills. It has
left us with a civilization that is no longer self-reliant. Most of our
population is unknowing and ill-prepared.

Losing these skills does not mean that we no longer need them. It
does not mean that we are no longer faced with problems, emer-
gencies, and natural disasters. It means that when these situations
arise, the greater majority will be blindsided and succumb to the
detrimental effects of what has taken place. More often than not,
we do not have the power to prevent every negative circumstance.
That is reality. What we do have is the ability to equip ourselves
mentally and physically with the proper tools to deal with those
circumstances when they are encountered.

We can see evidence of people suffering every day because of
forgotten knowledge and the loss of abilities which allow us to
persevere while under duress. Tragedy is still commonplace across

the globe. The indicators show that the struggle is widespread and often far more intense than it should be.

This is simply due to one major factor. The populace just does not know what to do when disaster strikes. The scary thing is that we watch these things happening to people every day on the television. We are aware of the potential risk. We know that it is commonplace. The obvious is laid out before us and yet for some reason many choose to put blinders on. This is a mistake.

In the military, we identify potential dangers with information and observation. Once those dangers are clear, we gather knowledge that can help us adapt. We train ourselves on the ways to deal with them and acquire the equipment that will be necessary for these situations. Why should it be any different for a civilian?

Natural disasters happen on every part of Earth without exception. Every time, the majority of people are not prepared. In recent years, natural disasters have displaced an average of twenty-five million people from their homes each year. That number almost doubles if you factor in the people who are affected by conflict zones. Amidst all of this, most people will do little to ensure their safety. It is just not clear why this is so. It seems unreasonable.

Simple Survival is for those who wish to separate themselves from the masses. It is for the individuals who are deeply interested in making an investment into their safety and that of their families. I hate to purvey a view with strong negativity, but that is how things are. Fortunately, this is where we can begin to make a positive change to the circumstances. Let's get started together.

DON'T LOSE YOUR HEAD

"Whether you think you can, or you think you can't—you're right."

—Henry Ford

MENTAL FORTITUDE

Certain scenarios call for immediate action, where the moments during shock and hesitation can mean life or death. Other times, diving in and doing the wrong thing can create a life or death situation where there was not one. Remember that knowledge and how you are able to use it will always be your greatest tool. What good is it to have all the equipment in the world without the ability to use it? Besides that, the things that you retain are always with you. They will never encumber or slow you down.

Knowledge will also bolster your confidence. That mental fortitude will help to ward off the common fears: I haven't been trained for this; I am not skilled in this area; what if I do something wrong? These are all real fears that will play with your mind in a dire situation. DON'T LOSE YOUR HEAD! You must be able to shrug these things off. Doing what you are doing now, reading, learning and practicing, will give you the right tools to battle the fear.

I can very clearly remember the first time that my platoon was engaged in an actual firefight while in Afghanistan. Real bullets are flying, and these guys want us dead! None of us have truly been in a live battle before. The enemy is shooting from rooftops and maneuvering around us. Flashes erupt in the darkness with heavy machine gun fire, explosions, and confusion.

I am with some of the best-trained soldiers in the world but do not think for a second that some of those fears did not pass through our heads. The fact is that they passed through and did not stay. For most of us, it was only a fraction of a second. Why? Simple. We had read about situations and tactics. We learned what to do and how to handle these particular situations. Finally, we practiced so much that our knowledge made us confident. The platoon was able to spring into action and do exactly what we needed to do.

All right, so most of us will never have to deal with bullets flying at us, but shocking things are happening all over the world, so you may want to at least think about it a bit. In truth though, taking in information, learning, and practicing, applies to everything we do. It starts in infancy and continues through the rest of our lives.

Think about it. Picture any one of the numerous abilities that you are able to perform with ease. Now, go back to the beginning. How good were you? Was there hesitation? Here is an easy one. Eating. Sure, we don't remember learning, but we have all seen a baby eat before. It is a complete mess. Food is everywhere. And now, you are so good that there is little thought required. The same process will hold true here and I promise you that it will not include food splattered across your face or involve the rigorous training that we used to get ready for battle.

SLOW IS STEADY AND STEADY IS FAST

Having mental fortitude will allow you to proceed in a Calm-Clear-Careful manner. This is crucial. It will help to prevent you from potentially making things worse. Imagine that a friend has fallen through the ice into freezing water. At best, he will have about two minutes before hypothermia sets in, and it is over for him. If you rush in to pull him out, it could weaken the ice further and result in you being in the same situation.

Pause and think. Calm-Clear-Careful. Is there rope or a long branch close by? Do I have time to get them? No. Take off your jacket and pull out your knife. Sleeve to sleeve your jacket should be about five feet. Get flat on the ice to spread out your body weight. Edge close enough to toss the jacket to him while holding the other sleeve. Set your knife beside you in case you need it to prevent from sliding when he begins to pull.

With your body and jacket, you should have well over eight feet of reach. Give him reassurance. Tell him to hold on tightly and kick with his feet to get his body flat on the water's surface. Then, pull to slide him onto the ice. If it breaks away, and he falls back in, back up closer to shore and try again. The more time that passes, the weaker he will become and the lower your chances to help will be. If you can get him out, remove the wet clothes. Dry him with some snow or your sleeve. Then, be kind enough to donate some of your dry clothes. If you are close to help, then go. If not, then you must start a fire immediately.

While preparing for Army Ranger School, I learned another way to address stressful circumstances. Fortunately, through knowing some of the right people, I was able to conduct part of my training with the Army Special Forces. One of the things that they forced into our heads was a great help. Slow is steady and steady is fast.

This is something that is commonly known by elite infantry and within the special operations community. Initially, this seems contradictory, but as you begin to understand how it works, it will make sense. Poorly trained soldiers will often burst into situations with high energy and rapid action. This type of response can easily result in confusion among the team and costly mistakes. This is likely to put you into a position that you can't get out of. I have seen this firsthand on the battlefield and it has a way of getting people killed. Trust me, you never want to be pinned down.

Slow is steady and steady is fast. If you watch a special operations team on a mission, their movements are smooth and methodical even when they are in the heat of intense action. Everyone is clear on what is happening next. There is seldom confusion and few mistakes are made this way. It is the same process that is taught for tackling big goals. Steadily working at it a bit every day until you finish. This technique will allow you to complete hard tasks much faster than using spurts of activity that lose time from hesitation and confusion in between.

MAKE A PLAN

Following this process, there must always be a plan of action. Every bit of previous knowledge and practice will make that plan more likely to succeed. Coupled with that plan you will tie in the resources at your disposal. Often craftiness, creativity, and ingenuity will be a huge help. There are almost always things that you can utilize to further your plan. It is best if you already have some of those things handy, which is something that we will delve into with the next chapter.

In most cases, there will be some time to formulate a plan, though that is naturally dependent upon the situation. With the situation above there were only a few moments. Generally speaking, it will be possible to give it some thought. Say you are stranded in the wilderness and you know what needs to be done. If you fumble about haphazardly from one thing to the next, you might just be setting yourself up for failure. Make a plan.

Prioritize the things you need to do by importance. There is rain coming and it is cold. You probably want to work on a shelter and find some dry material for fire. You are out of water, probably a few days from help, and the climate is hot and dry. You guessed it. Locate water. Or, you are in a favorable climate with fresh water but haven't had any food in days. Yep. It's time to get something to eat. I know what you are thinking. Well that is simple. These situations are often intertwined and quickly become complicated. Everything has a time and place and you need to prioritize.

We make plans every day and often don't even realize that we are doing it. Broadening the use of this activity is not complicated and is easy to refine with some focused thought. Also, remember that your plan is not something chiseled in stone. Don't be afraid to adjust it if variables rapidly change on you. Better yet, you see something coming and are able to make deviations before it becomes a problem. Another saying frequently used with infantry soldiers is "stay alert, stay alive."

This also translates very well to survival and everyday life. If you are able to identify problems in advance, you are afforded the opportunity to react as needed. Let's say that your plan is to take the family out to lunch. It's a nice sunny day so you decide to sit outside at the tables in front of the restaurant. While you're engaged in great food and family conversation, one of the drivers on the street is having a seizure and has lost control of his car. Unbeknownst to you that car is now heading off of the street and swerving directly toward your table.

How observant are you? Would you notice the situation and be able to safely get your family out of the path of destruction? What if this is taking place behind you? Could you have been seated in a better position? Stay alert, stay alive.

The plan can change at any time and often does. Because of these changes, it is good to note that a simple plan is often your best bet. Don't overcomplicate things or get bogged down in the details. How often do we put together an intricate framework in our head about how we believe things should go and then it all falls apart on us? That is life. You have to be able to "roll with the punches" as they say. The more that you can simplify means fewer odds for complication and it will be easier to adjust when the situation deems it necessary.

Be sure to include everything vital into the plan. Prioritize your focus, get the equipment or supplies needed, and take action! Everything else can be kept on the back burner. Using this method, the most important things will always get done first. Make a simple action plan every morning and it will improve your productivity and efficiency with whatever you do. Before long, it will be second nature when you need it the most.

THINK OUTSIDE THE BOX

Sometimes, in order to alleviate the problem facing you, a change in mindset is needed. At times the things that you may be faced with can be completely foreign and outside your realm of understanding. Other times you just need to tweak your thought process and look at things in a slightly different way. Reframing is a handy way to come up with a solution. One way of doing this is to think like a professional. How would an expert in this field act?

What if someone needs medical aid and you have absolutely no skill in this area? What would a professional do? Remain calm, call for assistance, and give reassurance to the person in need. It may not be much, but it will surely help.

How about wilderness survival? What would B.G. do? Okay, Bear Grylls is a personal hero of mine and knowing what Bear would do will undoubtedly be useful, but that is not what I am getting at. Who are the true experts in the wild? The animals. They are out there every day of their lives and they have all become specially adapted to overcoming the same needs that will likely plague you.

Though you will never have warm fur like a rabbit or be able to stalk prey like a cougar, there are many things that you can learn from animals and the ways that they stay alive. You can cover yourself with dry leaves or long grasses to ward off the cold and rain like a small rodent in its nest. You can eat some bugs to help sustain you in between better meals (just ask Bear). You can take note of what the animals are eating, where they find it, and how they manage to obtain that food.

You can turn up your senses and maintain awareness of your surroundings like your life depends on it. Stay alert, stay alive! You can adopt the persistence of an animal who often will only have a 10% success rate when searching for food. And you can accept that frequently surviving in the wild will mean sparse water, cold nights, days with an empty stomach, and weeks of drenching rain. The animals have adapted to living with it all and the list of things that you can learn from them is endless. Don't discount this.

Another way to think outside the box is to view the world through the eyes of a child. Children look at the world with a sense of wonder and amazement. They are extremely observant and will notice minute details that our experienced brain has mistakenly learned to tune out and become numb to. Any parent knows how often a child will stop you to look at something that you walked right past while trudging along obliviously.

A child does not think about dirt and spiders when they crawl into the small crevice under a toppled tree. "Hey, look a fort!"

they exclaim, finding a perfect shelter. Yet, all the while we are worried about grime and bugs. There is a long list of accounts where children have miraculously survived through unspeakable odds using these very skills. It would be wise to take a few tricks from their book.

USE EVERYTHING

Resources abound if you know where and how to look for them. It is not uncommon to be without some things that you might need. You must be able to improvise. Many of the tips above will aid you with this. Almost everything can be used in some ways that they were not actually intended for. Need something dry to get the fire going? Pull some fuzz off your socks or use the lint from your pocket. Need to stop someone from losing massive amounts of blood from an injury? Use a tampon for gauze and a strip of fabric from the bottom of your shirt as a bandage. Need to ward off a bear that comes into the camp where you are cooking? Bang your cookware together so the noise will scare it off.

Even a simple rock can have many uses. Don't have a hammer? Rock. Keep dangerous animals away? Rock. Protect your fire? Rock. Boil water? Rock. Sharpen a knife, spear, or another tool? Rock. Okay, you get it. I could write a long chapter on the practical uses for a simple rock. The point is that after thinking about it, one finds numerous things that can be used in irregular ways.

Don't forget that the other people around you can be your greatest resources. Often, there is one person with the presence of mind who is taking care of the situation. In the heat of the moment, they forget about those who stand by in a state of temporary shock watching everything take place. These people are critical assets. "Call the police." "Run for help." "Quick, I need your shoestrings." "Can you hold this?" "Go and bring the car." "Watch to make sure there is no more danger."

Even though you may be in a flurry of activity taking care of things, there are usually simple tasks that others can aid you with. Seconds or minutes can mean the difference between saving the day or feeling regret. Whether there is an emergency or not, things are always more efficient when everyone plays a part.

DIRT TIME

Dirt time is a term frequently used in the survival world. Essentially, this is where you will take the things that you have learned and actually practice the skill. Dirt time is a core principle when it comes to being adept. For example, one can read all day about riding a bike and watch hours of video where people ride bikes, but you will not be able to ride until the physical process of riding takes place.

All of this chapter has been about being prepared mentally. It is the primary key to unlocking success in anything you do. Refine the areas in this chapter where you have strengths and develop the ones that need improvement. Learning these things will help you in daily life. The more that you are able to implement them, the better you will become. Gather knowledge. Make a prioritized plan daily. Be more observant. Adjust your thought processes.

Use the dirt time to develop and expound upon the things that you learn in this book. Work on becoming proficient so that when the time comes you will be ready just like we were in our first battle. You are stronger than you know. You are able to endure unbelievable things. This is especially true when our mind is prepared, and you just refuse to give in. Remember that your brain is the best tool that you have. It will always be there to provide aid if you just let it.

PREPARE YOURSELF

"By failing to prepare, you are preparing to fail."
—Benjamin Franklin

As a youth, learning to carve out an understanding of survival was accelerated when I became a Boy Scout. The "Be Prepared" motto of the Scouts is right on the mark. It is something that I abide by on a daily basis and is some of the best survival advice you can get. Along with foundational lessons and fond memories, the Scouts became a great developmental proving ground when coupled with the forests of Wisconsin.

HAVE A KNIFE

I hate to be exceedingly redundant, but this is a point that needs to be driven home. Have a knife! Have a knife! Have a knife! Always have one with you and take it everywhere you go. This does not mean that you must haul around a huge beast of a knife. Get a good quality pocket knife and have it in your pocket, purse, or jacket every day. Just make it a habit. There is normally no legal problem with a pocket knife, but it wouldn't hurt to check the local regulations on size and restrictions.

If you take most survival experts and tell them that they are going to be dropped into a remote area of wilderness for an extended period with only one item, what do you think that item would be? The answer will almost unanimously be a good quality knife. With the proper know-how, all the things required to survive can be more easily obtained or constructed with a knife. In many tribes across the globe, the rite of passage from boy to man involved being sent into the wilderness to survive by using only his wits and a knife. I cannot overstate how critical it is to always have your knife.

I admit, most of the time it will only be used to open difficult packages, slice cheese at picnics, and overcome the excessive restraints that stand between a child and the box that their new toy came in. It won't be long before you become far too accustomed to having it.

There is practically never a time when I am without my knife. Over the years there have been a few instances where I have temporarily misplaced my pocket knife. After a few days, the absence of my knife becomes utterly frustrating because I use it so frequently. When I reach down to find that it is not there I am hit with the agitation of being ill-equipped.

Honestly, it isn't very often that I need my knife for something exceedingly serious but there have been times that I was sure glad it was there. Quite often, while out in the wilderness, there has been a real need for my knife. A couple of times, I have had to pull my knife out for protection though I never needed to use it. Those who prey on others are often weak cowards who are looking for an easy mark. When they see that knife and a determined face that shows you are not afraid to use it, they will turn tail and run almost every time. I will caution that, if you feel like you might need to use a knife for protection, you would be advised to get some formal training so that your knife is not used against you.

If you are anything like me, that knife will be coming out on a regular basis. It will see its fair share of use and abuse. Take care of it, but don't be afraid to utilize it as the tool that it is. Unfortunately, there will come a time when that knife reaches the end of its lifetime. Sometimes they don't hold up because it was not the best quality, or it will just end up breaking over time.

Other times they are good for years but after a while turn into something with loose locking mechanisms and a floppy old blade that has been sharpened so much that it will not hold an edge. I know that you have come to love it and the two of you have been through so much together, but it is time to let it go. You don't want to be stuck with a junk knife when you need it the most. Sure, a bad knife is better than no knife, but you want something dependable at your side. That is why you are carrying it after all.

You don't need to spend a lot of money on a reliable knife. I have hardly ever paid more than $50 for a pocket knife. Pay $300 for a top-of-the-line knife and you will baby that thing like a new sports car. The purpose is not to have something cool that you can show off to your friends. It is a tool that should be used to aid you. I will say that over the years I have bought disappointing knives and I have had great ones.

Make sure that you know the differences in blade selection and how they will work best for you. I prefer a thick drop point blade that is durable with a partially serrated edge for different cutting options. Also, look into the different styles of locking mechanisms and how dependable they are.

If you find a great knife that suits you well, go back and buy three or four more. One for your car, one for your backpack, and at least one replacement. There is nothing worse than letting go of that old friend and not being able to find a suitable match to replace it with. Trust me. I can still recall the best one that I ever owned. It had a fantastic surgical steel blade, was nice and thin for my pocket, and held up for years. Sadly, I only bought one and I still think about it every time I need to find a new knife. I wish I had purchased twenty!

Always keep your knife sharp. Over time, wear will set in and the edge will diminish. I can always get the sharpest edge by using a good old-fashioned sharpening stone. They are easy enough to find on the internet or at many sporting goods stores. A good stone should last you a long time. Many of them have a rough side and a fine side for finishing. Find one that is big enough to hold with your fingers comfortably out of the way. It will work better than a cheap small one and you will be less likely to accidentally cut yourself.

There are also the easy to use sharpeners that you simply pull the knife blade through. Most of them work well for a while and are cheap to replace. Another option is the sharpening steel that is frequently used by chefs and regularly comes with kitchen knife sets. You may already have one.

Read instructions and watch a few videos on whichever sharpener you decide to go with so that you know the best techniques. As with anything, make sure that the instruction comes from a reputable source. Amusing as it may be, don't pick the guy who is doing it for the first time and cuts himself in the process. Now, get some practice on those dull kitchen knives in the back of your drawer. They could probably use some love.

ON YOUR PERSON

Now that we are clear about the knife, there are a few other ways you should prepare yourself: First off, dress properly for the weather or bring something along in case things change and it turns ugly outside. You should never be far from fresh drinking water and if you will be, take an extra bottle with you. Have a lighter. It is small and easy to throw into your purse, backpack, or pocket. Last, is a power bar or small, nutritional snack. It's best if you find something that is non-perishable and packaged. If you are just out in town or shopping or running errands it is easy enough to just have these things in your car. If you are doing any kind of activity in the outdoors, then it is best to bring them with you.

There is a reason for these items and the order in which I gave them to you. There is something commonly known in the survival community as "The Rule of Threes." You can survive three minutes without air or submerged in freezing water. Let's hope that those two are off the table. You can survive without shelter in a harsh environment for about three hours. Proper dress will prevent early onset of death due to exposure and give you time to find decent protection or make a shelter with your knife.

Now, you can survive three days without water if sheltered from a harsh environment. That bottle of water can give you an extra day or maybe even two. I recommend a one-liter stainless steel water bottle. The lighter will reinforce the first two by providing heat from a fire and give you the ability to boil any water that you are able to collect in that steel bottle.

Finally, you can survive three weeks without food if you have sufficient shelter and water. Naturally, that power bar will not be able to last very long but it will offer some sustenance until you are able to find something more. Once again, the ability to make a fire will also help by providing the option to cook any food you may be able to gather.

There are other items that you can bring along on a day trip, especially if you are doing things outdoors or in the wilderness. i.e. hunting, fishing, hiking, cross-country skiing, biking, or boating. A small backpack or satchel has plenty of space to carry what you need. A sturdy rain poncho or tarp can be turned into a perfectly functional shelter if needed. One liter of water is the minimum but it is good to have more. Guys, beer is not a substitute. Toss a few extra bottles of water in that cooler. If you freeze them, it will keep everything else cold. A small first aid kit is a good idea too. Accidents happen. Miraculously enough fishing hooks constantly seem to make their way into things other than the mouth of a fish. A compass is never a bad idea. Having a small flashlight can also be important.

There was a time when I was living in Florida that I planned a short hike in the dunes of a state park. At the ranger station, I got a map and reviewed some trails with a park official who said that they were clearly marked and easy to follow. I selected a route that would take me about an hour to complete. It was midday and the sun was beating down so I applied sunscreen, put on a hat and grabbed my water bottle before setting off. I expected to have sufficient water for a short hike since the map also had a couple of water points indicated along the way.

The trail was easy to follow from the beginning but after about a half hour it started to get questionable. I started to notice various trails and paths that were not indicated on the map, and I was almost to the point where I would need to make a turn at an intersection. Walking in the white-sugar-sand was difficult with the reflecting sun amplifying the heat.

With a bit of luck and some confusion, I was able to correctly make my turn and find the first water point. My relief turned to disappointment when I realized that the water had been shut off. With about a half bottle left, I decided to press onward even though an hour had nearly elapsed. Farther on, the trail started to make a number of turns and it was crisscrossed with many others. Before long, the best use for the badly marked map was to fan my overheating body.

I knew that I was lost and nearly out of water but still had a general sense of direction. The dune grasses and scrub growth provided little respite from the sun which had become brutal by this point. Angry, I gave up on the trails and made a direct course for the main road that ran through the park. The hour-long walk that was recommended to me turned into over five hours of fatigue in the sweltering heat. That bottle of water, slight protection of the hat and sunscreen, strong physical condition, and a good sense of direction got me through the ordeal. Anyone who was not prepared could easily have become a casualty in the same circumstances.

Just remember to give some thought to where you are going and what you plan to be doing. It may only be a thirty-minute drive to a restaurant, but those thin clothes that look nice and flat soled dress shoes or high heels will be no good to you if the car gets stuck in the snow on a frigid winter night. Think about what you would need if the weather changed, something went wrong, or if an accident were to happen. Now take those things with you and everything should be fine.

IN THE VEHICLE

Just as there is a minimum number of specific items that you want to have on your person, there are also some things that should always be in your vehicle. This may be the car, truck, motorcycle, boat, moped, or even snowmobile and ATV. If you have all of them, equip all of them. For the most part, these items can be stashed in the glove compartment, console, or trunk until the time comes that you will need them.

Put in a spare knife for the off-chance that you leave home in a hurry and forget the one that you should be carrying. It will happen. You will also want to have a multi-tool to use for simple mechanical problems and numerous other things. Have some extra water and a lighter or two. Add some long-lasting food rations as well. Get a good medical kit that is more comprehensive than the small travel kit with just a few bandages and salve. Keep in mind that crashes involving motorized vehicles can be very serious and it might be a long time before help can get to you.

Other good things to have are as follows: a flashlight, gloves, jumper cables, 20 to 50 feet of strong nylon rope (550 cord), blanket (wool is best), and a tarp with long tie-down cords. If you live in an environment that gets cold, you will also want to add at least one larger size candle that is clean burning. If stranded in the car for a long time the candle will keep your car warm enough for you to survive. Note that if your environment also gets very hot, the candle can melt during summer so, it might be something to take out at that time. Wrap the candle in a big piece of aluminum foil and put it in a sealable bag. If you need it, the foil can be put into the cup holder and the candle is safe to burn. If there is a need to leave the vehicle behind, this candle can be very good at heating small shelters and monitoring the oxygen supply inside.

If you want to go a touch farther, which I would advise, keep a small backpack in your trunk as well. It works well for storing the items above and some extras. I have a military uniform in mine. Thin jacket, pants, boots, socks, shirt, winter hat, bandana, and a poncho. It does not have to be military, but they are rugged and often easy to get second hand. Any all-weather clothing that is durable will do. I also have a water filter, solar blanket, chem-lights, and a survival/medical and CPR pamphlet. You should have no problem packing everything in. If for any reason you need to abandon your car, the things that you need are available and can easily be thrown on your back when you need to move quickly.

AT HOME

The next level of preparation will be at your residence. In the house, you should have a larger backpack containing all the same items listed above. Okay, so leave out the jumper cables, but the extras that were listed above are a must. With the all-weather clothing in this pack, you will also want a heavier coat. Make sure to put in a compass and a map of your area. Another thing to have is an in-depth survival guide. I would be pleased if you choose to add my book since Simple Survival is a great foundational tool. Be aware that there is always more to learn and choosing a guide that is best suited to you and your area should be the main focus.

Also, have a hatchet and a sturdy tent that is just big enough for gear and you or your family. Have a case or two of bottled water on hand. You will want at least two five-gallon tanks made from plastic. One for water and one fuel just in case there is a need to travel with them. They can be put in the garage or near your backpack. You should keep at least a month worth of dry rations or non-perishable food as well. This does not have to be super expensive. Dry beans and rice are cheap and will go a long way, but you will need things of higher nutrient value to supplement them. As well as that, I would get a small duffle bag that can be used to transport all your medical supplies and basic hygiene items if needed. I will cover this to a larger degree in the First Aid chapter.

Many people will want to have a firearm. This can be important for protection and obtaining food. There is a lot that goes into that discussion which I will leave up to you. In the end, this will boil down to personal choice and the laws of the country that you live in. Many variables are involved in such a decision, but if it is the route that you choose, seek professional advice/training and follow all the safety precautions as needed.

SOMETHING FOR EVERYONE

If it is just you and there is nobody that falls under your care, this is not a huge deal, but that is seldom the case. If you have a family of six, that means there is some work to be done. Your spouse may have a separate car that they drive. Yes, you will need to square them away as well. If you have children, we can't forget that they have the same needs as you, if not more. Pets are just as fond of eating as we are. Don't forget them. This may seem daunting at first. Remember, prioritize and make a plan. Just like a big goal you can chip away at it one bit at a time. We don't want to leave anyone in need.

WHY ALL THIS STUFF?

Yes, it is a big list and if you are wondering, I do not hold any stock shares in survival equipment companies. The biggest reasoning here will fall under natural disasters. People talk about elaborate government takeovers, civil war, and things that seem far-fetched. I do not want to underplay the fact that there are places in the world where these things are actually happening. We have countries all over the world where the people are living in fear because of war or hostile governments. If that is you, then having prepared yourself with these items is paramount.

The majority of us can rejoice in the fact that we do not live with the shadow of these dangers looming overhead, but natural disasters do happen on a regular basis in nearly every corner of the globe. When they take place, everyone needs supplies and there are never enough to go around. Often, there is no warning of a natural event and you have no chance to get what you need. Be prepared.

We all know of the extreme destruction that can be wrought by hurricanes, earthquakes, tsunamis, and volcanoes. It is not uncommon for a tornado to devastate a town. Wildfires ravage many homes and vast areas of land every year. Dense populations have developed around lakes and rivers that are prone to massive flooding. Violent storms that quickly drop huge amounts of rain and contain powerful winds can arise almost anywhere. Even blizzards and ice storms frequently shut down many places and can leave them without electricity for weeks. Do you have the things that you need if one of these events strikes you?

DON'T SKIMP OUT

I know that when the spending of money is involved, people tend to get a big frown and squirm in their chairs uneasily. I also know that there are very few of us that can go out and buy a pile of gear without financial complication or a violent tongue-lashing from our spouse. Think of this as an investment in the safety of your family and explain the reasoning so that others understand it the same way. Better yet, have them read the book! These are things that may be needed to save lives and that is not something to take lightly. Some gear you will already have. Others can be purchased at second-hand stores for an affordable price.

Look at the areas that you are deficient and start to fill in the gaps with the items that are of the greatest importance. After a while, you will have the things you need. People may ask why you are getting all this stuff. Sometimes they do not understand the sense behind it. It seems like a lot of effort or you will probably never need those things, they might say. Don't let them hold you back. If you believe that there is importance in preparing for the safety of your family, that is all that matters. It is always better to have and not need than to need and not have.

While living in Florida, I was able to experience firsthand the chaos that takes place when a bad hurricane rolls through. The initial panic prompts a rush on the stores which are rapidly depleted. This is where the decent nature of people begins to break down. It's something that you do not want to be part of. Expectation of the destructive force causes a hasty evacuation. You will be well ahead of the masses if you are ready to move quickly with the things that you need while others scurry about hoping to find them.

Some will choose to hunker down and ride out the storm. Right or wrong, I was in this camp and decided to face the oncoming danger with my family. Honestly, I was less experienced at the time, and we did not have everything that we needed. After the hurricane went over the power was out, there was serious flooding and widespread devastation.

Amidst this havoc, some may have to get by on very little and in many areas, the lack of supplies leads to a general lawlessness and elevated danger for a lot of people. I was struck by the realization that many of these struggles could have been avoided. Quite some time passed before things were able to fall back into order. It was at this time that I began to seriously question people's aptitude for preparedness.

FAMILY EMERGENCY PLAN

While you work on obtaining supplies, there is one more thing that will be easy enough to do and should happen right away. Put together an emergency plan. Think about the natural events that happen in your area. If a tornado warning is put out for your town and you are at work while your kids are at home on summer vacation, do they know what to do? If your wife must get out of the house quickly and does not have a phone, is there a prearranged place where the two of you will be able to meet? Who can she call if she needs help and you are unreachable? If there is danger at home do the children know who to call for help when you are not there? Do they have a safe place to go if they need to leave the house or will they need to figure that out on their own? What if that person is not at home? Where do they go next? Will you know where to look for them or will you need to find them? What if there is a fire? Have you thought about it?

Have you talked it over? Go through these questions and come up with others that pertain to you.

Make a plan that involves the phone but do not rely on it. Have a backup plan as well. If parents or friends are part of that plan, then make sure that they are aware of it. You don't want your friend to head out of town because of danger but your kids are left behind because you never told him that they might be looking for his aid. Remember to include things like allergies. If you are allergic to bee stings does your spouse know where the medicine is? Would your child know how to help? Put together specific plans for different situations.

Have emergency contact numbers programmed into phones and written down in a certain place at home. Make sure that everyone knows the difference between times to stay at home and when to leave. Sit down and seriously think this through. You will want to write the different parts of the plan down and put it with the emergency numbers. It would also be good to put it in the notes section of family members' phones. People tend to forget things that are not reviewed on a regular basis, so make sure that it is readily available for reference.

FALLING BACK

For the most part, you can look at these different levels of preparedness in the same way that one might view a military unit that is deployed into a hostile area. I will explain this by working backward through the list. Think of your home as the base of operations. It is located in a relatively safe place and you have everything that is needed to comfortably survive there. Leaving this base to conduct missions, such as going to work and shopping, is a regular thing. Perhaps things get bad and you need to hole up in your home for some time. This is not a problem because you have gotten ready for that ahead of time by having extra food, water, medical supplies, etc. If for some reason disaster strikes and you are forced to abandon your home, it is time to fall back to the next level.

Now you gather personnel and move out in a vehicle. If you have time then, load the large pack from your house and any equipment that will be important and take it along. If not, this isn't the worst thing because some of what you need is already in your car. That car is also a shelter and a fast mode of transportation for passengers and gear. Let's say that now you need to dismount and leave that vehicle behind. Now, we jump to the next level.

With a backpack, you are able to haul a good amount of equipment and still move on foot relatively unhindered. You still have the things needed to stay alive and can continue the mission. If you were able to take the tent along it will provide good shelter, but you should at least have a tarp. There is always the chance that rapid speed is required, and the backpack is slowing you down too much. There might be no other choice than to drop down to personal equipment.

Now you are carrying what you can. It might be in a small pack, a bag or just your hands. Our priority of thought will have to become shelter, water, fire, and food. Knife. Small tent or tarp. Water filter and metal container. Lighter and ferrocerium rod.

Rations. Medical. Compass. Multi-tool. There is not much more you will want to get rid of.

The worst thing that could happen would be that disaster strikes and it is just you and the things that you brought along. We will just hope that you listened to me and have the proper clothes, your water bottle, the lighter, a snack, and that trusty knife.

GENERAL CONDITIONING

Much of this chapter was about equipment and strategic planning but there is also a physical element to preparing yourself. Maintaining a healthy body that is accustomed to regular exercise will always work to your advantage in an emergency situation. I'm not suggesting anything extreme, but you should be strong enough to haul a pack full of gear over extended distances if needed.

Naturally, there will always be limitations, but I have also seen people come up with solutions for almost every physical handicap. A man at one fitness center I went to would drive up every day and head into the pool to swim laps while I was lifting weights. After lifting, I would go to the pool to swim beside him for 45 minutes. Most days he was still at it when I finished and got out of the pool.

This may not seem entirely amazing until I tell you that this man had no legs! The way he climbed out of a hands-only driving car and unfolded his wheelchair before deftly pulling himself into it was cool. The laps in the pool . . . well, that just speaks for itself.

Healthy conditioning will give you extra strength to draw upon and help to stave off medical ailments and injuries. Another benefit will be an overall surge in your self-confidence which will weave itself into many aspects of survival.

DIRT TIME

So, now we begin to put things into practice. Make a list of the places where you are deficient. Fill in the gaps until your equipment list is complete. Start today with the small things. Remember the necessities. Shelter/Water/Fire/Food.

Watch the market for advancements in equipment. New inventions or better-quality gear could apply to your situation or environment. Test out new products that might be useful. Keep in mind that the items outlined in the chapter are just the basics. You can decide what is a comfortable level of preparedness, but it is always something that can be expanded upon.

Also, go to work on that emergency plan. Make sure to include alternatives and secondary precautions. Bring everyone on board so that the plan is seamless. You may still question the need for some of these items. That is all right. In the following chapters, you will start to learn what to do with the items that you have begun to prepare yourself with.

This might be the tough one but try to find some time for physical improvement. Pick an activity that you enjoy and start there. Incorporate more activities that are challenging or push your boundaries. Make it into a habit to stay healthy and active.

SHELTER

"A COMFORTABLE HOUSE FOR A RUDE AND HARDY RACE,
THAT LIVED MOSTLY OUT OF DOORS, WAS ONCE MADE
HERE ALMOST ENTIRELY OF SUCH MATERIALS AS NATURE
FURNISHED TO THEIR READY HANDS."

—HENRY DAVID THOREAU: WALDEN

ENGAGE THE ELEMENTS

There is much to be said about having a good shelter. Anyone who spends over a week in the wilderness with next to nothing will know that a deep level of appreciation for your home begins to develop. This is especially true when it comes to that cozy bed and a dry pair of socks! Facing the elements without shelter can be a severely demoralizing experience. While I pride myself in having the things that I need, there have been times that it just wasn't possible to fashion a legitimate shelter.

We had missions in the mountains of Afghanistan where we were out for several days at a time. To set up a camp was to give up our position and that was something we could not afford. Trying to get some sleep on a cold mountainside, exposed to the wind, and lying on a pile of rock is no fun at all. The only protection was a thin poncho liner and the warmth of the buddy that I gladly snuggled tightly against.

Many times, in ranger school, we faced prolonged exposure as well. They were trying to push our bodies beyond the breaking point just to see if our minds would be able to override the severity of the situation. We would go days on end being cold and wet, pushed to the point of exhaustion with very little to eat and almost no sleep. Our bodies were hardly able to respond. You would not believe what a person can withstand if you just decide to keep going. One lesson those days taught me very well is that the harsh elements are not your friends. One should do everything possible to prevent them from destroying your will to survive. Having a way to resist them is critical.

Shelter does far more than just keep the rain off your back or prevent the sun from stealing vital water from your body. When you have combined knowledge, materials, and the environment to create something that can protect your existence, there is a strong sense of accomplishment that comes with it. This is mentally uplifting and will help to provide a positive attitude. This, in turn, means that you are more apt to push on. It will also allow the body to retain valuable energy. Any time we struggle against the elements, energy is expended, and we burn up our resources. Survival and conservation go hand in hand.

Shelter will also help us replenish the body by giving it a better opportunity to obtain much-needed rest so that we can recharge for the next day. Comfort, even if slight, will relax one's mental state so that you are able to focus on the task at hand and not on how miserable you are feeling. Shelter will also arm you with a sense of security and protection from animals as well. Silly as it sounds, even a mouse can make a lot of noise in the darkness and when you are not sure what it is, that mouse will play games with your head. Any bit of separation between you and whatever may be lurking in the night will help to put your mind at ease.

LOCATION LOCATION LOCATION

Just as in the world of real estate or the placement of a profitable business, the site in which you choose to set up shelter is a huge factor to consider. In a rushed situation, it will just have to be the best place for the moment. For a flood or rising water, it will mean a stable place that is elevated. A tornado shelter will be somewhere low and protected. A hasty shelter might even be the middle of a lake in the case of a fire. Largely, those scenarios are easy enough to figure out. For the most part, this section will be about finding a place in the wilderness.

Survival is a game for the careful observer, since there are always things to be utilized. Often, the pieces of the puzzle are scattered about, and you will need to bring them together. That might mean that some of those pieces will have to be gathered along the way and taken to a suitable location. Rarely will you find everything bountifully laid out but, if you do happen come across the perfect spot for a shelter, take it. Even if it means losing some time by halting early, you will make it up later. This is because there won't be time and energy wasted while hunting for materials or rest that was lost due to an inadequate shelter. You will be better off in the days to come.

Here are some things to look for and others to avoid. High and dry is a good place to start. Low and wet areas become an interlocking chain of negativity when it comes to a shelter. They will often be thick with insect life and dense vegetation that is difficult to move through. Air pressure also causes the cold to settle into these places. You never want to sleep on wet ground and it makes fire-building overly difficult. While these low places might be a good place to search for food and shelter materials like reeds for roofing and long grasses to bed down on, you never want to make camp here. Using the side of a gentle slope or low hill work fine.

Building materials are always something to look at, especially when you do not have a poncho, tarp, or tent. It will be easier if some of these things are close to your shelter site. Whatever can be found that has been provided means less work for you and more focus on other things of importance. Most of the time it will involve some stronger branches for framework and supports. Find covering for the roof and walls to keep out the wind and rain, or sometimes the sun. Then, you will want something on the floor to separate you from any moisture and the ground which can absorb up to 80% of your body heat.

Pine branches, sticks, brush, logs, leaves, sod, grasses, reeds, sheets of ice, snow, broadleaf plants, ground, rocks, tree bark, roots, vines, and salvaged manmade materials all fall under the category of useful building supplies. Things like a downed tree can make a good place to provide natural cover and a support to prop branches for walls. Many of those branches can likely be taken from that same tree, and they may even have leaves or needles on them, which can stop the wind and rain.

Avoid any plants that are poisonous or cause irritation. Knowing the ones that are common in your area ahead of time is always wise. Check into it. Learn them and put the information with your survival guide. It will also be important when the time comes to forage for food.

The selection of your site should also include evaluation of the wind, sun, and shade. Your particular circumstances and climate zone will factor in a great deal here. The wind can be great for ventilation and cooling in a hot location. Conversely, that wind could rob warmth, eat through the wood from your fire, and push smoke into your shelter. There are places where the wind will change constantly, and this is hard to battle. Predominantly, it will follow a pattern that can be worked into your favor.

Remember that the air flow can be compared to that of water in many ways. It will channel through valleys and ravines, or open areas and clearings. Like the water, it will follow the path of least resistance but keep in mind that it will also push up or down through heating and cooling. These patterns are hard to notice at first because they must be felt through an understanding of their workings. It is only seen through secondary signs such as cloud movement, frost in a swale or the lifting motion of fog when the morning sun begins to heat the air. Over time, focused awareness will make these wind patterns more apparent to the trained eye.

The sun can be used for heating and drying out clothing or gear. It could also be the toughest enemy there is to face. In cold places, basking in the warmth of a sun-baked slope will be a pleasant reward from a well-placed shelter. Other places are so hot that you will need to confine yourself to the shade until cooler parts of the day or even the evening. This is not exclusive to desert environments. When energy and water conservation are a factor, the heat will deplete both if you are not mindful of it. Good judgment about when to be active and when to take shelter in such instances can be the difference between lasting one day or surviving a week.

If anyone might be looking for you, it will also make sense to pick a place with good visibility for both you and potential rescue parties. In hostile situations, concealment will be necessary, but in most events, this is uncommon. It is good to note the movement of animals where the shelter will be positioned. Being too close can provoke dangerous encounters or disrupt their movement. In the case of the latter, it might mean that you have diverted a vital food supply. Lastly, the close proximity to moving water can damper your ability to hear things of importance such as noise from animal movement, the thunder of a storm coming, or the calls from someone that has come to your aid.

There are also some dangers that are always best to watch out for. Anywhere that can be influenced by rising tide is bad. Ravines and dry river beds which can be rapidly flooded are risky at best. The high points of mountains and hilltops, as well as tall trees that stand alone, will attract lightning. Places where many trees have tipped over often indicates that the soil is weak, or roots are shallow. There is a chance that you could be crushed by a falling tree if winds become strong. Also, watch for dead trees or trees with big dead branches in the area of your shelter. These are called "widow makers" and you never want to find yourself under them. Check the area to make sure that it is not likely to be affected by an avalanche, mudslide, or falling rock. All these dangers are next to impossible to avoid at the moment they take place, and they claim many lives in the wilderness every year.

SIZE

When it comes to the construction of a shelter, it is important not to overdo it for a number of reasons. Small and simple is a good guideline. Overall, it should just be big enough for personnel and gear. More complex designs and bigger shelters can mean added problems. Something small uses less material to build. Less material saves energy and requires less effort to obtain. Together, this equates to extra time spent on other necessary activities. You can always go back and make improvements later. A little shelter means that there will be more materials that can be used for better insulation and waterproofing which can sometimes be difficult with a large construct.

A confined space will also heat more rapidly and hold the warmth longer. It is nice if you can sit up inside especially when there is a need to hunker down for a few days because of bad weather. Sometimes you will only be able to lay down in the shelter, but cramped and stuffy can work in your favor. If you think of the animals that build a nest or a burrow, it might be stuffed with things to keep them warm and dry, but that home is seldom oversized for their body. Keeping these things in mind, I will now go into some descriptions on how to build various types of shelters that you will be able to use.

HASTY SHELTER

A hasty shelter will be anything that you can come up with quickly. This does not mean that it will be bad or ineffective. There are times when it is not necessary to make something for the long term. Or, because of your plan of action, it may not be worth the time. In other instances, things like the weather or darkness might force you to make a hasty shelter.

With a tarp or a poncho, there is almost always something to tie the corners to. Use shoestrings, or a sweatshirt or jacket draw-string if need be. Sticks, rocks, or a log can be used to hold one end to the ground. If there is nothing, then just sit on one edge and drape the rest over you and your gear. That will be enough to keep you dry and a bit warmer. Here are a few options that you can choose from.

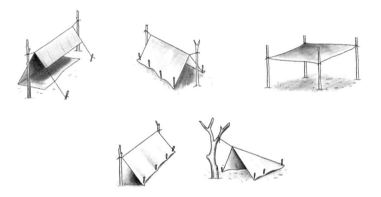

These hasty shelters are great with a poncho or tarp but will suffice, when made from something natural. Trees tipped over or standing are effective. Find an evergreen if possible. Most variet-ies offer better protection and readily available materials that are easy to gather. Collect some fallen needles, leaves, or grass to sit on. Wedge extra branches into the bows above you for overhead cover and put your back to the trunk for a wind block. More branches and leaves can be pulled in next to you for additional insulation. It will not be the peak of comfort but should take less than five minutes and will offer decent protection.

Crawling into long grasses or thickets of tightly packed bushes deliver very quick shelter from the elements and can give a surprising level of protection in a pinch. These places are favored by deer, rabbits, and many other animals. Don't be surprised if you have visitors but I wouldn't expect them to snuggle up and share their warmth. In these places, you must find the thickest spot possible. Gather up some covering for the ground. Then, pull in everything around and above you as close as you can get it.

A hasty debris shelter will also work if there are no other options. Pile leaves, grasses, or plant material together. Using logs or bigger branches to keep it together with a frame works best. Gather as much as you are able. Now, pretend that you are a kid again and burrow into the pile. Surround yourself as well as possible. Yes, you can expect some bugs, but this shelter will help to keep out the cold and hold back a surprising amount of rain.

It is good to note that any of the hasty shelter ideas can be combined to improve protection if the surroundings permit. Picture a tarp shelter under an evergreen that is growing amidst long grasses. Now, pile in some bedding and insulation for the walls. In a very short time, it can be easy to come up with an extremely functional dwelling if the natural settings are properly utilized.

LEAN-TO

There are many ways to make a lean-to shelter. This is often a solid choice because it is easy to construct quickly and, in most cases, very functional. Another reason for choosing a lean-to is the fact that they are easy to improve and modify as time permits. The basic form will often follow that of the hasty tarp shelter and can be built right over the top of your tarp for extra protection.

An open lean-to will begin with a strong branch placed horizontally between two trees or a rope tightly tied between them to form a ridge. The ridge can also be propped against something at an angle to the ground. The ridge might even be something that is already there such as a bigger log or partially supported tree that has fallen. Note the direction of the wind when preparing the ridge because this will factor into the location and construction. You generally don't want the cold wind blowing into your doorway or directly battering one side of your shelter.

If you have a tarp, it will be tied onto the underside of the ridge so that you can make an angled wall on the side that the wind will be coming from. Now, gather branches that can be propped against the ridge. When placing branches over the tarp, use care so that you do not puncture the plastic. It is best to keep an air space between the tarp and branches that make up the wall. This is better for insulation and keeping rain from seeping through.

For branches that will not break off easily, use your knife to make a cut around the place where you want it to break. Then, snap it off. Making this cut weakens the integrity of the fibers in the wood. This trick will help you gather stronger, green branches. Even branches as big as your wrist can be taken this way if you score the branch then, push away on the branch and cut deeper. Keep working around until it breaks off. Even a small blade will be a big help if used correctly.

Without the tarp, a steep angle to the wall will give you less room inside but it will be better for keeping the rain from dripping in. Be sure to select branches with some strength for this layer because it will have to hold the roofing material and possibly more branches. Also, put the branches close together and fill all the gaps. This will make it stronger and keep out the wind better. With scant materials or limited time, this may be as good as it gets for now.

If you have leaves or wads of grass, stuff the cracks between the branches on your wall. Next, you will want to put together some kind of insulation and roofing. There are a few options and it will depend on what is available. Sod or dirt with roots and plants works well but this takes time and is more complicated. The effort is generally not worth it unless you know that it will be long-term or there is nothing else to work with. Pine branches, broadleaf plants, bark, reeds, long grass, and leaves are more common and easier to gather. Take care when collecting grass and reeds. Wear gloves and cut them with your knife. Pulling with bare hands can give you nasty cuts that are easily infected.

Start from the bottom edge and go across in a row with the roofing material. With pine boughs, grass, reeds, and plants you will want to put them upside down in bunches, so the water runs down off of them naturally. Then, add in another row that overlaps the first. The layering will keep out the rain. Think about the roof of your house. If you only have grass or leaves, there may be a need to add extra branches onto the outside so that it all holds together. Remember that you might be using a combination of these things. That is fine. Not having enough of one kind of material for the entire roof is not irregular. Just work in whatever you have with the same layering effect.

The last part is the ground covering. More is better here. While something soft is always preferred, don't rule out a layer of small branches. Sticks of the same size that are lined up next to each other work fine. These may be slight on comfort, but they will be effective at keeping you from the grounds moisture and its heat draining ability. Use a log or rocks to hold it all in place. Make sure that whatever you use is on the inside of the ridge. This will help prevent drips and splashing rain from coming in.

I have slept many nights on the ground and used all these different ground covers for bedding. I have also had the misfortune of going without. In the coldest of winter, a thick pile of long grass has helped to keep me nice and warm while sleeping soundly. Respectively, lying on the bare ground in warm climates, I have shivered the night through and barely slept at all because of it. Get something underneath you.

IMPROVED LEAN-TO

The next best thing that you can do with that lean-to is to add in another side to give you the A-frame structure. If you know that the time and materials are readily available, the branches for the second wall can be put in right from the start. I recommend finishing the side where the wind comes from before working on the other. That way if the weather changes there will still be partial protection. Also, at the peak of the ridge where the two sides come together, drape grass, reeds, or plants over both sides to cover the gap in the ridge. A branch pressed down on the top can hold everything together.

Add Roof Covering

Now, if the lean-to has two open ends, you can close the one that will not be your entrance by using the same process. If rain is a factor, it might be prudent to dig some trenches for drainage or make sure that the ground is sloped away from your shelter somewhat. In a cold climate where you have snow available, covering the structure will add a great deal of warmth, but you may need to add extra branches to support the heavy load of the snow. You don't want all that work to come crashing down on you in the middle of the night! You can place some branches or hang an extra piece of clothing in front of the door to close it off more. Otherwise, pull your pack or gear in after you are inside to help block the opening.

SNOW SHELTERS

Popular winter sports and activities often lead to people being stranded in harsh weather without help. Every year, people die in the back country due to snowmobile breakdowns, getting lost while skiing, injuries, and isolation due to snowstorms. Depending on the situation, it could take up to a few days or a week before you are able to find help or get out. Without some kind of shelter, one night—or even a few hours—in freezing temperatures could be enough to kill. Do whatever you are able in order to stay warm.

Winter can sometimes be more challenging for shelters, especially when the landscape is barren. Snow can bury workable materials and make them obscure. There will generally be less plant material. In the forest or wooded places, it should still be possible to put together a lean-to that is covered with snow and well-insulated. At times there is just not a lot to work with. When this is the case, the first priority will be finding a wind block of some sort. A stand of shrubs, depression in the ground, or small hill might be the best that there is. With luck, there will be some brush, grasses, or dead plant stalks that you can utilize. Don't get discouraged. There is still a lot that a person can do to keep from freezing.

Sweating in a cold climate can be a killer. Walking, gathering materials, and shelter-building with heavy clothing on can cause the body to rapidly overheat. Sweating will deplete your body of vital fluids and make your clothing wet. After the work, your body will cool, and the combination of wet clothes and cold temperatures can be extremely dangerous. Open your coat, take off inside layers, or work less vigorously. It would be completely foolish to build a perfect shelter then, freeze to death inside of it because you got all wet while doing the work.

SNOW TRENCH

The snow trench can be a very fast shelter to build if there are some materials at hand. The main thing that is required for this shelter will be something to support a roof covering. Without this, you will need to choose a different shelter. You will also want to have snow that is at least ankle-deep, or it will be difficult to make a trench. Deeper snow is ideal.

First, dig a rectangular trench that is about double the width of your body when lying down and long enough to put gear at the entrance near your head. With less snow, it will need to be gathered and piled on the sides of your rectangle. The depth should be twice as high as your body at a minimum. Remember that this measurement will start at the top of your ground cover. There must be enough room to slide in and roll over easily while the shelter is covered. Once the trench is in the right dimensions, fill in the ground covering and bedding. Pine branches are perfect for this. If there are none it might mean that you just need to dig under the snow to find leaves or plant material.

At this time, it will need the framework and roof support. Branches work well for this, but many other things can be used to improvise here as well. Skis and poles, long snowshoes, or a removed snowmobile seat/engine cover can all suffice if need be. Note that the improvised roof coverings will normally only help if you also have a tarp, poncho, or something to drape over them. If you have gotten this far with the improvised coverings and there are no other natural materials, this will be about the best you can do with limited time. Even a good roof made from branches should be covered with a tarp, but it is not necessary when the right natural materials are available. Cover the edges of the tarp with snow to hold it in place.

Now, cover the whole thing over with pine boughs, smaller branches, grasses, leaves, or plant stalks. This will help to prevent snow from falling inside if there is no tarp. It will also give some added insulation and strength to the roof. When this is done, spread a generous layer of snow over the entire structure. The amount will depend on the strength of the roof that you built. Don't overdo it and cause a collapse. A solid roof should be able to hold quite a bit of snow if you formed it properly.

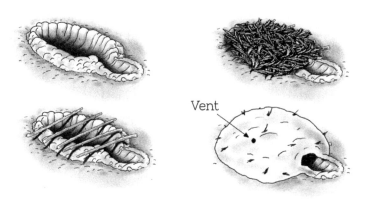

A fresh supply of oxygen is critical for any kind of snow shelter. If it is fully sealed, the heat from your body and breathing will form a thin layer of ice on the snow which will stop air circulation.

While you are asleep, suffocation will slowly shut down your brain and cause death.

With ventilation holes poked in on each side, the shelter will be complete. If there is snow falling or drifting, make sure to keep these holes open regularly. If you have a candle from your vehicle, this can also be used to give extra heat and monitor oxygen supplies. If it has trouble staying lit or goes out, then you need more ventilation. Pulling gear in to block the door will help seal out the wind.

SNOW CAVE/DRIFT SHELTER

When there is a large drift or deeply piled snow, digging out a cave shelter can prove to be an effective solution to having a lack of materials. If dealing with hard snow this can be more time-consuming, but it will often be warmer and more comfortable than the snow trench. When snowdrifts form, the particles of snow will generally bind to one another and develop into a solid form. These drifts and deep piles are excellent for shelters. Improvising something to dig with will be beneficial. A stick or knife will work if there is little else. Even a small bundle of branches or tough plant stalks held together will do. A rudimentary tool can speed up the process and help to keep your fingertips warm.

Chop into the drift or piled snow on the side that is away from the wind to form an entrance. Once you are inside, begin to dig laterally by turning at a right angle. Making the door at an angle will help to keep the wind out. Begin to clear out what will be your shelter area. Keep the opening just large enough to get in and work. A smaller entrance will be easier to block up when you are finished.

Clear snow from the top down with a smooth curved form to the roof. This way, there will be less stress from the added weight on your ceiling. Also, if it caves in, you haven't invested the time and effort into a lot of digging. Be careful to leave a thick enough layer on the ceiling so that you don't break through or weaken the structure too much. It should not be less than the distance between your elbow and wrist. As you dig your way down, keep a smooth, rounded form like a dome. This shape will have a stronger natural support and the smooth sides will cause water droplets to run down to the edges and not drip on you.

When clearing out the snow, pile it strategically so that it will better block the wind. Do not put it on top of your structure. This could cause a cave-in. Once you dig closer to the bottom, it is best to leave a flat sleeping area on one side. Keep the sleeping platform raised at least one hand-width above the ground. Alongside the sleeping platform, dig a deeper path that leads out to the door. The deepest place should be the doorway and trench leading out. This depression is called a cold sump. When you are in the shelter, the cold air will settle into the lowest area and keep the sleeping shelf a bit warmer.

At this point, it will be time to gather some ground cover. Laying on the bare snow will cause it to melt and your clothing will get wet which is a seriously bad thing in a cold environment. Make sure that the bedding is placed far enough from the outer wall so that you are away from the drips that run down the sides.

The last thing needed is ventilation. With a stick or your knife, carefully drill out a hole in the back of the ceiling. The size of your index finger and thumb together in a circle is about right. If snow accumulation is a factor, then it might be best to go out the side of the shelter with this hole.

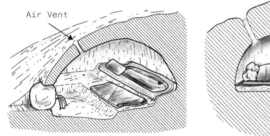 

A rolled ball of snow or chunks of packed snow can be used to block the entrance. A backpack or any extra clothing can also close off the space. Once it is sealed, a properly constructed snow cave will maintain a temperature that is 32°F (0°C) or warmer. This temperature should hold even if the outside temperatures fall to -40°F (-40°C).

QUINZHEE

Its name originates from the indigenous people of Northern Canada and Alaska who spend almost their entire lives in the cold and snow. The quinzhee is a great winter shelter when there is basically only snow to work with. It is a strong shelter that can be made into larger dimensions when there are several people to accommodate. In the right conditions, it will also hold up for a long time if properly constructed. The downside is that the quinzhee will require a great deal of time, effort, and snow. Unless there is no other choice, it wouldn't be something a single person would build for a one-night stay.

You will almost always need something to gather snow with for construction. It would take a very long time to collect enough with just your hands, but it is possible. To start the quinzhee, you will need to keep throwing snow onto a pile. For one person, it should be at least waist-high and longer than body-length from toes to fingertips when outstretched. The pile can be round or oval in shape. If there are four people in your group will need to be a much larger pile that is nearly twice that height or more.

Now you will want to add markings over the top so that there is evidence of where to stop when excavating the ceiling from the inside. There are a couple ways of doing this. In most cases, it is done with sticks poked into the pile. Break fifteen branches at a length that is about the distance from your elbow to the tip of your thumb. Scoring the branches with your knife will allow you to break them in specific places and give more accurate measurements.

Poke one stick into the top of your pile just enough so that it will stay in place. Now, take four more sticks, and do the same thing on each side. Leave about the same length sticking out of the top for all of them. Now pack snow around the base of your sticks to make them more stable. Next, you will need to pile on more snow so that it reaches the top ends of your sticks. This will be the thickness of your roof and walls. The other ten sticks can now be poked in around the rest of the pile. This will give you enough indicators to gauge off of when clearing out the snow from the inside.

There is always the chance that you do not have any sticks to utilize. At this point we get creative. You will need to mark the top of your original pile with something. Use grass, leaves, small rocks, or even dirt. Simply place these items sporadically over the pile in a layer that will be clearly identifiable when digging the shelter out. It does not have to be completely covered. Now, layer the pile with more snow and try to keep track of the depth so that you maintain at least that elbow to thumb measurement. When in doubt, make it thicker. There will be less chance for collapse which is far more likely when the roof is thinly made.

This stage is very simple but extremely critical. Leave it alone. The snow pile must sit for about 90-180 minutes. This is a process called sintering. While the snow was being gathered and piled, you inadvertently brought snow of different temperatures together and they became mixed. When piling them atop one another, a compressing effect also takes place.

These two things cause the molecules in the snow to bind with one another and freeze into a hard mass over time. In extreme cold, this process takes place faster, while in temperatures near freezing, it will require the full three hours. To skip this part of the procedure could prove to be a fatal mistake. This is normally a good time to check the list of priorities and continue progress. Fire preparations will likely be high on that list.

After the sintering has taken place, pick the side that is protected from the wind and carve out an entrance that is just big enough for the largest person to crawl through. Keep the entrance low to the ground so that cold air settles there when the shelter is finished. Once inside, begin to carve out a work area that you can fit into. It is recommended to dig while on your knees so that if the structure were to cave in, you would have an air pocket to breath and can exert more force to push your way out.

Digging slightly upward and clearing some of the roof out first will take pressure off the structure. Be sure to watch for the gauge sticks or markers. Keep the shape of the roof like a dome. As with the snow cave, a flat roof will not hold and can fall inward. Make short walls on each side of the entrance with the snow that is cleared out. This will add extra protection from the wind.

As you clear out more of the lower portion, make sure to leave the sleeping platforms raised above the cold sump. Two people can sleep together on one platform for added warmth. With four people a platform can be put on each side. The cold sump is then channeled through the center of the shelter. Smooth out the roof and sides into a uniform dome. Etch in small channels where the edge of the wall and sleeping platforms meet to catch water that runs down.

Now, it is time to add the ground cover to sleep on. Once that is done, you will need to remove a gauge stick at each end of the shelter for ventilation. If there were no sticks, then chisel some holes. Once again, there will need to be some kind of block or ball of snow for the door when you are inside. The inside of this shelter will easily stay above freezing in temperatures that drop to -40°F outside.

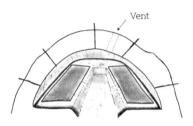

Vent

SWAMP/JUNGLE

I put the jungle and swamp shelters together because, in both cases, it is most important to construct a bed that is off the ground. This means that the shelter will involve similar elements. In each of these environments, moisture, insects, and animals are a danger to avoid. Not having a place to dry yourself in these places will also cause the skin on your body to deteriorate rapidly. This will lead to open sores and you will then be vulnerable to all kinds of disease and infection.

I have dealt with this before. After spending just over a week in the swamp without a chance to properly dry off, the skin on my feet was rotting off and toenails were falling out. I know this is not a pleasant visual and trust me, it is terrible for your morale. I knew that I would be in serious trouble before long. Those of you who are feeling remorse for my feet can rest easy. Fortunately, I was able to dry them out and they healed normally This is the harsh reality of such a place. Heed the caution because it is not something anyone wants to go through, especially in a survival situation.

The insect and animal life here is an altogether different problem. Due to warm temperatures, available food, and plenty of water, there will generally be an overabundance of life in these places. Many have bites and stings that will deliver poison or serious irritation. Know that most of them can traverse the ground and trees alike but keeping yourself off of the ground will give you a better chance to avoid potentially dangerous encounters.

I have spent a fair amount of time in the tropics and vast swamp-lands over the years. I have suffered through the nasty stings from fire ants and bites from spiders. There have been run-ins with alligators and poisonous snakes. During my training in the army, I was stung in the hand by a scorpion when getting up from a firing position on the ground. It was rather painful. The swelling and numbness made it difficult to use that hand for two days. Survival here leaves little room for error. In some instances, these encounters can mean the difference between life and death. Even many of the plants here are equipped with thorns and carry toxins that are harmful or deadly. Slow down. Be aware. Use caution.

TREE PLATFORM

Sometimes the quickest and easiest way of making shelter in these places will be to simply find the right tree. If you are on the move and will only need a shelter for one night, this is the most logical solution. Strapping yourself to a tree with a poncho overhead may not give you the best night's sleep, but it will work in a pinch.

A tree with the perfect crook or branches that spread out at the same level can work well to your advantage. Tying a tarp to an overhead branch will also provide some rain cover. The picture below depicts a simple perch that is best suited for speed and ease. Note that this tree design can also be made into a more functional shelter using the instructions in the next portion.

SWAMP/JUNGLE BED

For this shelter, it is prudent to begin with the construction of a raised sleeping platform. The rest of the shelter will be added to fit around the bed. If there are salvageable materials that can be made into a hammock, this will be your best option. A hammock is fast and will require the least amount of work. It will also be better at keeping out animals and crawling insects. If you have a heavy canvas tarp this will be better suited for roofing. Don't use it for a hammock unless there is sufficient roofing material as well.

The main requirements for building a sleeping platform are stable trees that are preferably not large in diameter, sturdy poles or branches that can support your weight, a number of shorter branches that are strong enough to lay on, and some kind of lashing or cordage that will not break when holding everything together.

Workable material in these environments is readily available to a large degree. Living branches or bamboo will be superior choices since anything that is dead begins to rot quickly due to the moisture. Dead and rotten branches will not be strong enough to hold you.

Use rope or salvaged wire to tie with or search for natural cordage. A lot of the time there will be vines, roots, or fibrous plant material that will work. Test it for strength and flexibility first. It does not need to bend enough for a knot but must wrap around the pole and tree without breaking. A raised shelter will involve a fair amount of cordage, so be sure to gather some long lengths when you find it.

There are a variety of different ways to build the sleeping platform. I will explain three of them. Each has positive and negative qualities and your situation will ultimately be the deciding factor.

The four-tree method is very stable, but it may be hard to find the right trees in a proper configuration. It will also need a fully constructed roof when you do not have a tarp. The three-tree method is less stable, but the tree configuration is much easier to find. It will also need a full roof, but this will be harder to build because of the triangular shape.

The two-tree method is also less stable, but you can almost always find two trees that have the right spacing. Here you will have to make two support poles that the sleeping platform will attach to, but they will also double as your roof supports. This can save you some time. The form of this one will cut down the space on your sleeping platform and put you close to the roof which could mean that you have a better chance to get wet if the roof is thatched. This shelter works well with a tarp for roofing which alleviates that downfall. These are not the only ways to build a sleeping platform but, in most circumstances, they will prove to be the most functional choices.

I will focus my description on the four-tree method but by looking at the illustrations it will be easy enough to make the necessary changes to construct the other two. First, locate trees that are spaced in the form of a rectangle that is just a bit longer than your body and wide enough to lie down on comfortably.

Two long poles will need to be lashed on each side running the length. They should be at least waist-high but extra height will afford added protection if you are able to get in and out without too much trouble.

Your poles can be placed on either side of the tree to make adjustments to the shape if needed. When lashing the poles, use the crossover and loop-around pattern. After going around at least four times, the overlapping friction should hold things together well. More lashing will add stability. Finish by tucking the end under the last loop and pulling it snug. Make sure to test the strength. One corner does not need to hold your full weight but should be close to being able to do so. If you have trouble with this, try to put some extra support poles on the underside and lash them in place.

Once all four corners are secured at the same level, it is time to add the crossbars that will make up the platform. You will want their length to overlap the support poles by the width of your hand on each side. These do not absolutely need to be lashed into place, but if the cordage is available, this is recommended. Moving on the bed can cause them to shift and fall out otherwise.

Without the cordage, you must make sure that the last crossbar wedges all the others tightly between the trees. If cordage is not a problem, then lash it together. The wrap is easy and can be done quickly when all the crossbars

Support Pole →

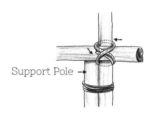

are prepared ahead of time. This will also make the whole thing more stable and give spacing which will provide better airflow to keep dry.

It is now time to add in the roofing for the shelter. Once again, having that tarp or poncho will save you a lot of time and effort. Without it, this will likely be the more complicated portion of this shelter. The roof will need a pitched frame that is secured over the sleeping platform. Fortunately, this will not need to support as much weight.

The downside is that with a roof over a raised bed you will have to work from off of the ground at some point. In most instances, this will mean standing on the sleeping platform. Take care when standing on the platform because all your weight will be on one point and not dispersed as intended. You may need the extra supports under the areas where you will be standing over the long poles. Move them as you work in different areas. Once the frame is made, it will require lateral bars that will be used for securing the thatch. The amount will depend on the size of the thatching material.

In the tropics, there are many broadleaf plants that can be used for roofing. In the swamp, reeds and long grasses will often be the best choice. Take something that is plentiful and will cover a large area. Tropical plants such as the elephant ear (Colocasia), banana, and many palms have leaves that are large and can quickly cover your whole shelter. In the swamps, long reeds can cover the roof in two or three layers sometimes. More covering offers better protection in these places where rain is frequent. Do the best with what you have. This could be a lot of work with smaller material. It is always better to be prepared with at least a poncho.

The thatching process can be complex and lengthy. Without the right materials, it will be downright frustrating, and you can expect to get wet. I will show a couple of basic variations here that are less complicated. There are countless ways to thatch a roof. Depending on what you have to work with, creativity and ingenuity could play a big role here.

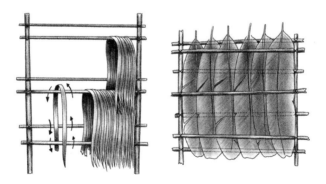

With the larger leaf plants, the lateral bars can be spaced evenly across the frame and you will be able to do a simple over and under weave. When using reeds or long grasses the lateral bars should be set in pairs with a small space between them. Here the reeds will wrap over the third bar from the bottom and then come back down to be tucked over and between the lower pair of bars. Use small bunches when doing this so that the coverage is thick and fits snugly into place.

IMPROVED JUNGLE/SWAMP BED

If you know that this shelter will need to be used for a longer period of time, then it could be wise to make improvements for better comfort and protection. While less important in warmer climates, you may still want to add some kind of covering that will soften the feel of sleeping on rough branches.

Walls can also be connected to the shelter and thatched in the same way as the roof. Salvaged material might also be an option. If you do add walls, it is best to end them just below the sleeping platform. If they go all the way to the ground then, you have just created another way for insects and snakes to reach you.

ARID/DESERT SHELTER

There is a right and wrong time to work on a shelter in a hot and dry climate. The heat of the day when the sun is overhead will be the time for you to seek shade and keep cool. This shade could come from vegetation, a rock outcropping, or the backside of a dune. A poncho that is secured to any of these natural formations will be far better. While waiting out the hottest portion of the day, it is prudent to do any other important activities that are possible.

This shelter is basically a replica of the snow trench that utilizes the sand or rocks instead of snow. The purpose here is to create a space that will protect you from the heat. Digging a trench into the sand will get you into the insulated ground where it will be cooler. If possible, you should find a location that has some building materials and will offer natural protection from the sun. In the dunes near a beach or body of water, there will be more things to work with like driftwood and plant materials. Arid climates will usually have a lot of rock and different types of scrub brush to use. A flat desert that is primarily sand will be the most challenging.

After finding a suitable location, the trench will first need to be excavated. It must be the length of your body with a ramp to slide in and out of. Make it wide enough to move comfortably inside. With dry sand, you may have to use rocks or branches to keep the sides from caving in. Pile the contents that you dig out around the edges to build up the height of the trench sides. It should be deep enough to lay on your side without your shoulder being higher than the top edge of the trench. You should try to find something to dig with. A strong branch or flat rock can be helpful. If the ground is just too hard to dig into, then use rocks or branches to build up a barrier in the correct shape.

Now, it is time to make a shade covering for the top. This is another instance where that tarp or poncho could be a lifesaver. This is especially true in a sand desert where there is nothing to work with. The sides can be secured by covering the edges with a layer of more sand or rock. If the tarp is big enough, it is best to add another covering above the first one. There should be a space between them that will trap an insulating layer of air. This can be done by folding the tarp in half or using another piece of material. The air pocket will decrease the temperature inside dramatically.

Without an artificial covering, you will need to depend on your surroundings. Get creative. Branches with grass over them will work. Poking scrub brush into the top sides of trench and leaning them together overhead will offer some shade. Stretch clothing across the gap if possible. Improvised covering can also be used in conjunction with a single layer of tarp if needed.

When there is absolutely nothing to use, the trench must be narrow and deep. Also, make sure that the length is heading in a north and south direction. This will not protect you when the sun is at its highest point but, there will be some shade on one side or the other for the rest of the day. Most of these climates are located closer to the Equator. Digging the trench to face east and west will mean that you are exposed to the sun for the entire day.

Air Space

DIRT TIME

Shelter-building is one of my favorite survival techniques to practice. It is always interesting because there are many variations that can be used to fit the location. The ability to integrate separate styles together gives you a multitude of possibilities. There is always something new to learn when working with improvised materials in different climates. I suggest going out in your area during the different seasons and working on the shelter-building skill.

Before you begin to work with the shelters, be sure to get some practice with the different knots pictured. Learn how to tie them and get accustomed to the jobs that they can perform. Being familiar with knots will come in useful for many aspects of survival. Using them for your shelter will help you understand how they work. Once you have a solid grasp of these, there are many others that can also be handy in the right circumstances.

Round Turn with Two Half Hitches

When you are ready to tackle some of these shelters, bring a tarp, fine rope (like 550 cord), a pair of gloves, and your knife. Once you get better, try to challenge yourself. Take only a knife and construct a good shelter with whatever is available. This will force you to think creatively and you will greatly improve your proficiency. Want to see how well you have done? Sleep in it. It is all right to have some comforts at this point. A nice sleeping bag is always great but if you truly want to test yourself, minimal comforts will be the best way.

If you have kids, nieces, or nephews—take them along. They will love this activity and the skills they learn from the dirt time will be priceless. You might even be surprised by some creative insight that they can lend to the project. Not only that, but there is great value which comes from the bonding that forms when creating something together. Just go out and make the important practice of this valuable skill into something fun.

Clove Hitch

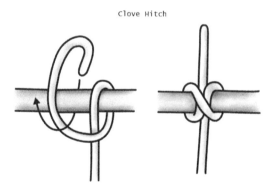

Square Knot

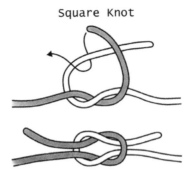

Secure ends with half hitch

Bowline

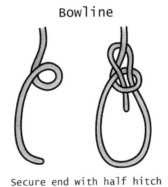

Secure end with half hitch

Figure 8 Slip

WATER

"WATER IS LIFE'S MATER AND MATRIX, MOTHER AND
MEDIUM. THERE IS NO LIFE WITHOUT WATER."

—ALBERT SZENT-GYORGYI

In favorable circumstances, a properly hydrated individual will survive little more than three days without water. Far less when facing intense temperatures and lack of shelter. Our bodies are comprised primarily of water, that is subject to continual loss, therefore, it must be frequently replenished. On average, we lose one to three liters a day. Sweat, breathing, digestion and bodily functions all contribute to this loss. When in a survival situation, finding water, consumption of water, and water loss must always be accounted for. Many times, it will take precedence over the other necessities on our list. This need is persistent and will require attention on a daily basis.

RETENTION

Our first defense is to protect the reserves that we already have. Good decisions and simple actions can make a veritable difference. If heat and pounding sun are a factor, this is the time to take shelter. Find a cool place that is shaded. Do not overexert yourself and cause excess sweating. Never lie directly on the hot ground. Clearing away the soil on the surface will reveal a cooler area below. Breathe through the nose at a slow and even pace. Talking and respiration from the mouth will work against you.

Eating should be kept to a minimum. Digestion will draw fluids from the body and cause the need for excretion which will take even more. Foods containing high protein and fats are the worst culprits. Processing alcohol demands fluids from the vital organs and will always cause more harm than good. Energy drinks and soda are also not a recommended choice for rehydration. Caffeine is a diuretic and the high concentration of sugars in these beverages pulls water through the kidneys that cannot be reabsorbed. Smoking dehydrates you as well, so save cigarettes as tinder for fire-building.

When water quantities are sparse, sip from what you have and consume it over time. To guzzle large amounts will dilute the bloodstream and it will be lost through the kidneys. When you are dehydrated, too much water in the stomach can also cause nausea and vomiting which is a severe waste of fluids. Stay away from drinking any unpurified water as well. Bacteria can produce sickness that will lead to diarrhea and vomiting. This combination will quickly put you in a dire situation.

WATER COLLECTION

Fortunately, water is one of the most abundant resources on the planet. Because we are so dependent on it, most of the population lives in proximity to water. Finding a continuous source is the best scenario and you always want to look for more water before you run out. Incidentally, you may find yourself in some of those places where water is scarce. When this is the case, you might need to rely on numerous methods of procurement. There are various bits of knowledge which can improve your chances.

Initially, the properties of water will give us some clues as to where it can be found. We know that it runs downhill and collects in low-lying areas. It is also subject to evaporation, so we must look in places that are protected from the sun's rays. Seek out valley bottoms or the base of hills and ravines. It is known that water is held in the earth. Dig in the lowest points of a dry pond or the outside bends of drained riverbeds.

After evaporation, it is returned in the form of rainfall. Be ready to capture it with a poncho or tarp when it does. Large plant leaves can also be used to catch or funnel rain into containers. Even laying out clothing to soak up rain can provide ample quantities. Rainwater will also become trapped in the depressions of stones or rocky terrain. If gathered from a clean surface, rainwater will not need to be purified.

The needs of plants reflect our own, so any places with gathered vegetation will be a good indicator. In areas that water is slight, these patches of green will contrast the surroundings and should be easy to pick out. Some plants that live in dry climates will store plentiful reserves of water inside. In Africa and Australia, the baobab tree holds vast amounts of water and has been used for thousands of years. Search the tree, and you will likely find a tapping hole that has been used by natives for generations.

This tree is endangered, and the thick bark should not be tapped unless it is a complete emergency.

A succulent dollar bush can be pressed to get bitter juices. It is recognizable by the flat round leaves. You can also obtain fluids by cutting off the top of a barrel cactus and squeezing the fleshy insides. This fluid will have a milky color which, as a rule, you should avoid, but the barrel cactus is an exception. The prickly pear cactus also holds a lot of moisture in the reddish yellow fruit and the flat ears of the plant itself. Cut away the spines of the cactus before handling it.

Soaking up the dew that collects on non-poisonous plants is another superb way to gather water. In the morning, use a piece of cloth to absorb dew from green plants and wring it out into your mouth or a container. Surprisingly, these small drops can add up to a decent amount in a short time. Sometimes the crevice between two trees that separate near the trunk will collect water that can be taken to boil.

In the springtime, maple and birch trees can be tapped for fluids. Cut a V shaped gash into the trunk with your knife. Cut past the bark and slightly into the inner tree. When the sap begins to run out, insert a small stick to direct the fluid into your container.

Warm sunny days after a cold night will be the best time to tap a tree.

Vines with rough bark are generally a good source as well. Follow the vine to the highest place that you can reach and cut a notch with your knife. Now, go to the bottom and cut the vine off where it comes out of the ground. The notch on top will let air into the vine and increase the flow of liquid from the bottom. Collect what drips out, unless it is sticky, has a milky appearance, or is bitter tasting. The sap or juices taken from plants should not be kept more than twenty-four hours or it will begin to ferment and spoil.

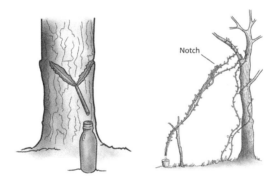

In the tropics, many plants will naturally catch water in their broad leaves or it will be held in reservoirs at the center of brome-liads. Banana and plantain trees can be cut down at the base of the trunk and when a hollow is cut out of the trunk, the roots will fill fresh water into the hole. Discard the first three fillings—as it will be too bitter—but after that, it will be potable. Cover the trunk to keep the bugs out and it will last up to four days.

The milk from unripe green coconuts is good. Mature coconuts contain an oil that will act as a laxative and this should only be consumed in limited amounts. They can be a precious food source. Get coconuts down with a forked branch, climbing or dislodging them by throwing other coconuts.

Bamboo can provide for you as well. Bend over a couple of green stalks and stake them to the ground. Cut off the tops and water will drip from them during the night. The hollow trunks of older bamboo will catch water if it has a crack in it, but it will need to be purified. Palms, such as the buri, coconut, sugar, and nipa will drip fluid when one of their lower fronds is pulled down and the inner tree is exposed. They will also bear liquid if the tip of a flower stalk is cut off.

Banana   **Bamboo**

The juices can be taken from many kinds of fleshy plants. A lot of different roots will also give water when the bark is stripped off, and they are pressed or fluids are sucked out. It is critical that these plants are positively identified and known to be free of harmful toxins. The best way to remove the water from many living plants is to create a solar still.

You will need a plastic bag or a plastic sheet that can be folded over and sealed. A plastic tarp, tent material, or poncho can work for this process. It is best to have clear plastic so that the sunlight can penetrate the bag and draw more water from the plants. Fill your bag about half-way full of vegetation. Tear apart broad leaves and make sure that there will be nothing to puncture the plastic. A rock inside the bag will keep it from blowing away. Fill the bag with air and seal it tightly.

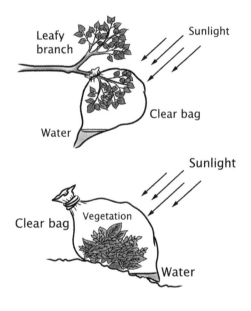

Now, place the bag into direct sunlight. Condensation will form on the plastic and run to the bottom of the bag. Do not let it leak from tiny holes that may be in the bottom. Place the hole over a container if this is a problem. Replenish the plant material as needed. This can also be done by tying the bag directly onto a leafy branch so that the water collects in the corner of the bag.

Animals and insects can point us in the right direction when we watch for the signs. Herbivores are generally not far from a source of water, especially larger grazing animals that habitually drink in the morning and evening. Look for droppings and find game trails. Heavily trodden paths where other trails converge will regularly lead to water if followed downhill. Carnivores are not good indicators.

Grain-eating birds tend to stay near water and will drink in the mornings and evenings. Watch to see how they fly. If heading to water, their flight will be low and direct. After drinking, birds will move from place to place and stop frequently to rest. During migration, many water birds will head for bodies of water or marsh areas in the evening when they stop to rest for the night. In the morning they can be seen and heard leaving these places.

Observing the patterns of certain insects can also be exceptionally reliable. Bees make their hives close to a dependable source and do not often fly more than a few kilometers from water. Ant colonies rely on water and following a steady column of ants can reveal a hidden cache. It may be a small crevice or notch in a tree that might require a strip of cloth to soak it up. This can be a huge windfall in arid climates. Normally, you will not find a fly more than a hundred meters from water, so they will also indicate that you are close.

Our bodies require elevated levels of water in cold climates. Paradoxically, our thirst and desire to drink is driven down in these places, so it is important to maintain hydration. Gathered snow and ice should be boiled. Cold temperatures will not kill bacteria. Melting ice is preferred over snow. It will yield more than double the amount of water and require only half of the heat to do so.

If you are melting snow in a metal container over direct heat, it is best to add the snow slowly until there is a decent base of water in the container. Otherwise, you will scald the bottom of your container. Clean, freshly fallen snow will not need to be boiled but it is best to melt it first. Eating snow requires extra energy to process and cools the body. Both things will deplete valuable calorie reserves.

Coastal ice will become desalinated after about a year and will begin to have a bluish color. After two or more years this ice will be almost completely free of salt. Grey or opaque sea ice will contain too much salt to safely drink. Ice taken from glaciers, rivers, and lakes has been used by natives of the polar regions for thousands of years. These sources are still relied upon by the indigenous people of the frigid arctic regions.

When you are stranded at sea, there are not a lot of options for fresh water. Seawater should never be consumed without desalinating. To do so will speed up dehydration. If this is continued over time, the body will progressively weaken from poisoning. The end result will be madness and death.

Capturing rain at sea should always be taken advantage of. Heavy dew is common and can be soaked up or gathered from the air with a sail that has some slack in the bottom to catch the dew when it runs down. If you have a way to boil the salt water, the steam can be collected on the underside of an angled plastic sheet so that the condensed water runs to a collection point.

With the right materials, it is also possible to make a solar still at sea. A large and small container can be used with a plastic covering. Put some seawater in the large container and place the small container in the center of the larger one. The small container will be empty so make sure that it does not float or move from the center. Cover the large container with the plastic and seal it by tying the edges. Put something weighted in the center so that the condensed water will run down the inside and drip into the small container.

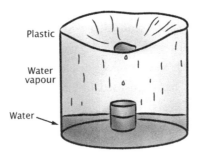

Plastic

Water vapour

Water

In many cases, fish will be one of the best sources when it comes to replenishing fluids at sea. Fish contain high levels of water in their bodies. As a rule, ordinary-looking fish with normal scales and fins will be safe for consumption. It is recommended that you pass on anything that has an irregular appearance—especially when in warm waters.

The juices can be obtained by cutting the fish into pieces and chewing out the liquids. If eating is not an immediate requirement, spit out the solids and use them to catch more fish. You can also put the pieces of fish into cloth and wring out the liquids into a container. Many larger fish will also have a water reservoir near their backbone that can be tapped and drained.

DECONTAMINATION

Finding a source of water is not a huge complication most of the time. Often, the problem will be locating water that is ready to drink. Dew, water from plants, freshly fallen snow or rain, and that taken from fish or the eyes of animals, are the few places that you can get water which will not need to be made potable. There is no guarantee, though. There are many rumors surrounding drinkable water, but the bottom line is, that there is no dependable way to determine the safety of water outside of a laboratory. To drink contaminated water in a survival situation will most likely lead to sickness that, without immediate rescue and medical attention, could edge you dangerously close to death.

It is easy to believe that a source of water should be safe to drink from. This lie will become more acceptable as your thirst grows and you become desperate. That crystal-clear mountain brook might contain the carcass of an animal rotting upstream. The most pristine lakes and rivers are still full of microscopic protozoa, bacteria, and viruses. Waterborne diseases account for approximately three and a half million deaths every year. Be smart, be safe, and survive. When it comes to life and death, look at every source of water as contaminated.

Even those listed above can pose some risk if they come in contact with the wrong surface. On a microscopic level, it only takes one drop. If you don't believe my warning, take some time to do a bit of research on a few topics: cholera, cyclosporiasis, dysentery, hemorrhagic fever, typhoid, Guinea worm disease, cryptosporidium, gastroenteritis, giardiasis, hepatitis E. This list is surely not complete, but it will hopefully be enough to knock out any doubt that you might have.

Before taking water from a source, it is best to do a visual inspection. Look for oil on the surface. Be sure that there are no dead animals nearby. When there is no green vegetation, or you see bones present, it is a safe bet that it is poisonous or dangerously contaminated.

Aside from boiling, few of the water treatment methods will be fully effective at removing all pathogens. This will require a metal container to boil in and the ability to make fire. If you came prepared with a container, filter and the means to build a fire, then you are in good shape. There is varied advice on the boil time, but to hold a rolling boil for ten minutes will provide complete reassurance in any circumstance.

There could be times that you need to improvise a container to boil in. This could be made from wood or something that cannot be moved over a fire. Use the primitive method of boiling with fire-heated stones placed into the container of water.

Boiling does not get rid of any chemical contaminants that may be present but in most wilderness locations this should not be a critical issue. It will not remove particulate either, so you are still dealing with dirty water. The dirt will not hurt you, but it is understandably not favorable. When possible, it is recommended that the water is filtered before boiling.

FILTERING

The filtering process can range through a spectrum that begins with primitive simplicity and ends with the inclusion of modern science. In its most simple form, this will remove large pieces of sediment and plant or animal matter. The most technologically advanced filter is able to clear out particulate, protozoa, bacteria, and most viruses. Even the best portable filters will not take away chemicals and heavy metals, though.

To simply separate larger debris it is possible to slowly pour water through layers of grass and a piece of cloth. By itself, a handkerchief can catch quite a bit of sediment. After this, let the water sit for about an hour. Much of the fine silt will settle to the bottom. Carefully take the top three-fourths of the water without stirring up the sediment. Depending on the source of the water, it could very well have a brownish color due to tannins that are left from decayed plants. Do not worry about the color.

A better filter can be made with a plastic bottle, sock, shirt sleeve, or separate layers of cloth that are tied to a tripod framework. I will explain how to make one with the bottle because it will better ensure that the water is forced through the filtering agents

and does not just bypass them by soaking through the fabric. If you do not have a bottle, use the illustrations below and the process will be the same. The second choice would be the series of cloth catch-basins and a tripod.

A larger plastic bottle or jug will give you the ability to process more water. If it has a cap, poke a few holes in it with your knife. Now, cut the very bottom of the bottle off. If the mouth is large and you do not have a cap it might first need a couple of sticks set cross-ways to block it up somewhat. On top of that, you can place a bed of moss, grass, or cloth. Over the bed, you will place a layer of partially crushed black coals from a previous fire. The coals can be covered with a layer of dry sand.

Now, add some larger pieces of coal. It should be topped off with a good layer of small pebbles or the coal will want to float when you add water. With a couple of holes in the top edge and some cordage, you will be able to suspend it above a container to catch the end product. Slowly pour water in the top and continue to refill the filter as it cycles through.

It is also possible to use something called a ground filter. This can be exceptionally useful in swamps, marshlands, or near a saltwater coast. Find a spot that is above the water line and dig a hole that is about elbow deep and just as wide. Water will begin to seep through the ground. Let it fill and then take from the top where it is clearer. Near the coast, you must be above the high tide line. Freshwater is lighter and should settle above the saltwater line. Stop digging as soon as you see water seep in because a deeper hole will give water with a higher salt content.

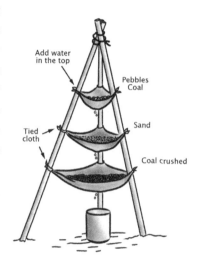

Add water in the top

Pebbles
Coal

Sand

Tied cloth

Coal crushed

Something similar to this is a below ground still. A hole should be dug in a sunlit area and should not go all the way down to the water line. At the bottom, you will place a container in the center where the condensed water will drip. Like the solar still, you can also situate vegetation around the container to add extra moisture. If you can salvage some plastic tubing from somewhere, this can be added to the still so that you do not need to take everything apart when the container fills up.

Cover the hole with plastic so that it hangs down in the middle like a funnel. The edges will need to be covered with dirt or rocks so that the plastic does not fall inward. A stone in the center will direct the condensed water into the container. Dirty or stagnant water can be poured onto the ground near the sides of the hole. This water will be filtered as it seeps through the ground and adds moisture to the still. When using vegetation, it must be changed every few days or it will begin to rot.

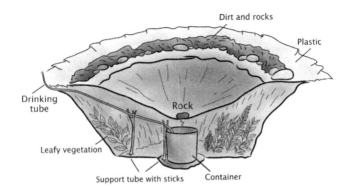

When it comes to portable filters, there is a multitude of options and the technology is changing every day. Some use ultraviolet light, adsorptive filters use a special magnet to attract contaminants. The various types of micro-filters trap material as the water passes through. All of them have positive and negative attributes. This market is constantly seeing changes and improvements.

My best advice is to do the research and read reviews before purchasing. Figure out what type of filter will best suit your needs, as there are many choices. Look at the capacity of water it will filter. Make sure that you know how it works and what specific contaminants it will remove. Depending on your needs, it could be prudent to have three different filters for separate locations. Think about your day pack, car, and home.

Many portable filters will not remove viruses, and depending on which part of the world you are in this could be a major factor. I prefer to use a filter in conjunction with boiling to be on the safe side. When dealing with dirty water, it is good to prefilter with primitive means or let the water settle.

Particulate will clog or slow down most filters. Using cleaner water will expand the lifetime of most portable filters and improve their efficiency. Note that when the water inside certain types of microfilters becomes frozen it can destroy the capability of the filter's integrity.

CHEMICAL DECONTAMINATION

There are a number of different chemical agents that are commonly used to make water potable for drinking. Many of them have been in use for a long time and others are new to the market. Usually, these are good at killing viruses but cannot always be relied upon to destroy protozoa. Again, this is an area where you will need to check the facts if you believe that this might be a good option for you.

One good thing about most of these is the fact that they are compact and easy to put into a small survival kit. Keep in mind that when using chemical decontaminants, the dosage must align with certain proportions. Not enough additive could prevent it from working and too much could make you sick. Often these agents do not work instantaneously and will give an unpleasant flavor to the water. Make sure to fully read instructions before use. In the right place, these can be a good thing to have.

SALT

A minute intake of salt on a daily basis coincides with the importance of water. The body requires about 10 mg of salt to regulate fluids. It is consistently lost through sweat and urination, therefore must be replaced. In hot weather, our reserves are depleted even faster. When the body is running low on salt, you will have a hard time quenching thirst. It will progress to weakness and lack of energy.

Next, there will be muscle cramps, dizziness, and nausea. The body will feel very hot and dry. Watch for these signs in yourself and other survivors. Upon recognition, dissolve a pinch of salt into one liter of water. Fluids, salt, and rest will be the fastest means of treatment.

It is not a bad idea to have some salt tablets or a small bottle of coarse salt with your survival gear. Most modern foods and survival rations have plenty of salt added to them for flavor and natural preservative. Wilderness food that you gather, on the other hand, will be largely deficient. Tribes across the globe have used animal blood as a solution to this problem for ages and still do today. Animal blood is rich in valuable minerals and a viable source of salt.

Small amounts of seawater can be added to your fresh water in a ratio of about one to eight parts. Seawater can also be evaporated, and the crystals gathered afterward. Salt is also obtainable from the roots of hickory trees and nipa palm. Boil the roots until all the water evaporates and then collect the black salt crystal deposits.

DIRT TIME

Now that we understand the importance of boiling, it is imperative that you obtain a reliable container for this process. Tackling water challenges without it will be exceedingly difficult. As a companion to that, investigate different filter options and find something that is right for you. Once those items are checked off the list, it will be time for some practice.

Think about your climate zone and the places that you travel to. What are the bits of knowledge that are most pertinent when it comes to locating water? If you spend time at sea, apply what you have learned and expound upon it. If you live in an arid environment, train yourself to find those hidden water sources. Everyone would do well to seek more information about the plants in your area that can provide for you. Also, take the time to closely observe the indicative patterns of animals and insects. When times get tough, these are huge windfalls and should never be discounted.

Now that you have learned more about meeting survival needs in your area, start testing the techniques described in this chapter. Construct each of the different types of still. Try to start from scratch and make a functional filter. Make the fire to get the coal. Find a bottle in the wilderness or use a sock. Gather the different materials for the layers that make up the filter.

Identify and extract fluids from the correct plants. On paper, the pictures and descriptions are not a big deal, but you will find that by working through these different procedures, it will pose certain complications. These complications will refine your skill. You will learn tricks to

improve your technique, find out how much can be gar-
nered from different plants and determine the amount of
water that can come from an efficient still.

Water needs will often be the biggest obstacle that you
need to overcome. To master these things is a huge
accomplishment and one of utmost importance. Take
great pride in your ability to prevail over this stage in the
survival process.

FIRE

"NEXT TO KNOWING HOW TO DRESS WELL, FIRE IS ONE OF THE MOST IMPORTANT BUSH SKILLS THERE ARE BECAUSE IT IS ONE OF THE FEW MEANS AVAILABLE TO MAKE UP MOST GREAT DEFICIENCIES."

—MORS KOCHANSKI, BASIC SAFE TRAVEL AND BOREAL SURVIVAL HANDBOOK

From the core of the Earth, and the beginning of time, fire has had a hand in shaping the landscape. Lightning creates fires that cleanse environments and make way for fertile rebirth. Destructive yet nurturing, fire has the power to control the delicate balance between life and death and should be widely respected.

Early humans borrowed natural fire and turned it into a vital survival tool. Over time, they were able to master that tool and gained knowledge that allowed them to start fire on their own. Through the centuries we have continued to use that fire and it can be attributed to a huge portion of our advancements. Take a look around. You will find that there are few things which we have created that have not felt the touch of fire. We have come a long way by harnessing this powerful force.

FUNDAMENTALS

Knowing where fire has brought us, the relevance here leads us back to the beginning. There is a vast array of factors which make fire crucial to survival. It adds dimension to shelter, water, and food requirements. Through heating and drying, it extends the survivability which is provided by the things that shelter you. Fire gives you the ability to boil water that could not be otherwise consumed because of harmful bacteria. It also gives you far more choices when it comes to sources of food. Many things just can't be eaten without first being cooked or boiled. Not only that, many food items can be dried or smoked to preserve them for later use.

Fire is a huge component when it comes to morale as well. It gives you a sense of control over your environment. It will offer security by lighting up the darkness and helping to ward off dangerous animals. You can use fire to shape and form different tools to aid your situation. It is also highly important when it comes to sending a distress signal. A lone person in the forest is almost impossible to identify from the air but even from a long distance a plume of smoke is quite easy to spot.

SIZE

The chosen function of your fire will determine the size that is required. Conservation of materials is always an important factor. Many native tribes had plentiful supplies but, as a general practice, they made a habit of only using what they needed. Do not squander your resources. A small fire can supply a great deal of heat if you have properly constructed it in the right location. Unless the cold is extreme, warming fires normally do not need to be much bigger in diameter than a dinner plate.

If you are going to use the fire for cooking or boiling water, you will need to maintain a higher temperature for a prolonged time. In most cases, this will require a larger fire with a base of coals. Connect your arms in a circle in front of you. This is about the right size. A signal fire will need to be prepared ahead of time. This will be a big fire that ignites rapidly. Most of it will consist of dry leaves, grasses or fine material that produces smoke. Once it is burning, throw on green foliage. There are seldom times when survival will require a roaring bonfire.

PREPARATION

When it comes to starting a fire, your success is hinged upon the ability to make the correct preparations. There are times when there will only be one chance to get it right, so this key instruction cannot be ignored. To begin with, one must understand the fire triangle. Think of each side of the triangle as an integral part. Those parts are heat, oxygen, and fuel. Without one or more of these, your fire will go out every time.

Take note of wind when it is time to start a fire. It will help to bring oxygen to the fire but too much is a bad thing. Strong winds will draw the heat away and voraciously eat through your wood supply. A protected place is desirable and will be more effective when it comes to heating and cooking. Also, be sure that the smoke will be drawn away from you and the shelter. Smoke inhalation, especially inside a shelter or confined space, will cause carbon monoxide poisoning and can be deadly, even in small quantities.

When a good location is found, stand over that spot and spread your arms apart. Mark the approximate distance. Use this diameter to make a circle on the ground from which you will need to clear away all flammable debris. If the ground is wet or snow-covered, you will need to make a raised base out of green wood or rocks. Do not take rocks from the water or very wet areas. When they become heated, the moisture inside can expand, and there is a chance that they could explode and cause injury.

When the ground is dry, it is best to dig a small depression and make a fire ring with rocks. This provides some wind protection for the fire and will keep it contained. After the fire has burned down, hot stones can also be taken into the shelter to provide a safe source of radiant heat. Be mindful of areas where the soil consists mostly of peat or fine roots. These places can start massive underground fires that have been known to smolder for years.

Now, it is useful to make a covering of dry material where you will start the fire. There is generally, some residual moisture in the ground and a layer of separation will increase your chances of success. Dry leaves, grasses, or pine needles work nicely. They will also give fuel to the fire when it is starting. At this time, you will ready the tinder, kindling, and fuel. All of these must be gathered and ready before lighting the fire. It is a common mistake to light the fire without collecting enough kindling and fuel. It could easily lead to a cold night (or much worse).

TINDER

Tinder is any fine material that will ignite with little effort. It should light with only brief contact with a flame or spark. In almost every case, it must be completely dry. Tinder should burn fast and create a lot of heat that will be able to ignite the kindling. It is wise to think about finding tinder well before it is time to start the fire. In a wet environment, this can save you a lot of time and trouble.

Many types of tinder can be gathered and dried as you travel or conduct other activities. There are often suitable items that you will come across while working on your shelter. Put them into a dry pocket so your clothing and body heat will draw away any excess moisture from the tinder. There are so many things that can be effectively used for tinder that it is hard to make a complete list. I will add some of the more common natural and man-made tinder. Awareness and thought about your particular environment will certainly yield far more things to use.

Natural:

- moss
- lichen
- old beehive
- leaves
- partially rotted wood
- fallen pine needles
- wood powder from insects
- feathers
- dry grass
- small rodent nest

- fine plant fibers
- bird nest
- wood shavings
- termite mound pieces
- shredded birch bark
- dry palm fibers
- shaved cedar bark
- fur or hair

- dry mushroom
- pulverized tree bark
- spider web
- down plant seeds (milkweed, goldenrod, cattail, dandelion, thistle, cotton, fireweed).

Man-Made:

- paper
- unraveled twine or rope
- charred cloth
- string
- cigarette filter
- pocket lint
- gunpowder from opened bullet
- tampon

- fine plastic screen or mesh
- seat cushion foam
- sponge
- automotive filters
- shredded carpet fiber
- helmet padding
- separated seatbelt material
- pulled fuzz from socks
- fleece or woven fabrics

Separate and fluff up any fibrous tinder to create layers of air between the combustible material. This will make it more likely to ignite and give you a larger area of flame.

Dry coals from a previous fire can be one of the best things to include with your tinder. The charred portion of partially burned wood is very receptive and will quickly become a strong ember. Crushing it will make it much easier to light a fire when using a lens. If you need to travel after a fire burns down it is always a good idea to take some cooled coals with you for the next fire. This tactic was a common practice with many native tribes around the globe. It will speed up the process every time.

It is good to mention that there are a few accelerants that can be used with tinder for either lighting or fueling the flames once they ignite. Gas or pine resin can be mixed with tinder to help it ignite but should only be used in small proportions. Once the tinder takes flame it is best to have some extra tinder to add in so that the flames keep going.

With this additional tinder, you can also add accelerants such as shreds of plastic, drips of oil, broken-up Styrofoam, pine resin, shredded rubber, and seat cushion foam. Larger strips of birch bark are a superb choice because the oils inside the bark will allow it to burn while wet. Use extreme caution when using many of these accelerants or artificial forms of tinder. Breathing the fumes from these things is highly toxic. Stay upwind and tie a cloth over your face.

NOTE: Please be kind to the tree when gathering birch bark. Take small pieces of the outer bark from numerous parts of the tree. Peeling back thick portions of the bark can expose the tree to harmful insects or disease. Cutting deeply or stripping large portions of bark will kill the tree outright. It is best to collect pieces from the ground or deadfall. Many times, fallen birch wood will rot away and leave plenty of bark behind for ready use. Thanks for helping to ensure that these resources will continue to service the needs of the future.

KINDLING

This intermediate wood will begin to give substance to the fire. Once again, you will be looking for material that is dry or very close to that. It is usually best to avoid things that are laying on the ground. They will tend to sap moisture from the soil and will be harder to light. Take dead twigs right off of trees or bushes. Sometimes dead branches fall and get caught in the trees or parts of them are not touching the ground. These will be good as well. If it has been raining, seek out kindling in protected areas. Sticks will often be drier if taken from the tree trunk on the side that is opposite of the rain. Search on the underside of bushes and thick growth. Sometimes deadfalls will have dryer wood underneath as well.

Use the snap test to check for dryness. When you break the twigs and small branches they should make a crisp snap. If they flex and bend without breaking easily discard it for later use. Another way to test for dryness is to touch the wood to the outer portion of your lip. You should be able to feel moisture if it is not dry.

I regularly divide my kindling into three piles. The first will be tiny twigs. Dead branches toward the inside of evergreens are a great place to look. Birch trees often shed small branches that are quick to take flame as well. Gather a generous bundle. The next pile will be anything that is up to the size of a pencil. After the twigs are burning these will be put in a few at a time. These sticks will begin to form small coals and create more heat. This pile will be bigger than the first.

The last pile of kindling will consist of pieces that are about the diameter of your thumb and slightly larger. As you add these to the fire, there should still be portions remaining from the first two piles. Using all three together at this stage will ensure that the fast-burning materials do not diminish too quickly and leave you with smoldering sticks. This is a crucial stage and it is still easy to lose the fire here. Get what you think you will need in the three piles and then double it.

PROCESSING WOOD

This next portion will require more rigorous work and the use of your knife. Always wear gloves when doing any kind of work that could damage the hands. Your hands are vital to survival and in most cases, they are not prepared for the abuse that you will need to put them through in the wilderness. Any protection is good, especially when working with a knife. When you cut, do so in a motion pointing away from yourself. To cut into a branch with your knife please place it onto something other than your knee. We haven't gotten to the medical chapter yet!

In a situation where everything is wet, there are a few things to try. Take the driest branches that you can find. Now, use your knife to shave off the bark and outer portions. The inside should be drier. You can also make "feather sticks". Take your knife and partially shave up portions of the stick but instead of cutting them off, dig deeper and leave them on the stick. Continue to do this on the whole stick. Make a bunch. These will catch flame more easily and should work even if they are slightly moist.

In some wet places, it will be hard to find small branches that are not soaked through. To catch flame from the tinder you may just need to make larger shavings from a big piece of wood. After that, you will need to split off small pieces to take the place of your kindling. Using a pocket knife with a folding blade is not recommended for splitting wood. There is a chance that it could break, and that knife is far too valuable as a tool. You must heavily weigh the need for fire against the potential usefulness of that knife. For this reason, I always have a full tang knife in the emergency pack that I put into a vehicle. If there is no other choice—be extremely careful so as not to put too much strain on the knife.

To split wood with a knife you must use the baton method. Find a solid hardwood stick that is about wrist-size in diameter. Break it off at elbow-to-wrist length. Now, shave the bark off one end of the baton. You will also want another stick that follows the same proportions as the baton. Whittle one end of this stick into a 30-degree wedge. This splitting wedge will be more effective and serves to protect your knife from damage. Place your knife blade on the wood where you want to split the piece off. Only take off small pieces. This technique is not designed for splitting logs unless you are that crazy person who carries a super hardcore beast of a knife.

With a folding blade, you will want to tightly hold the base of the blade where it connects to the handle. Use the thumb and forefinger to grip the flat of the blade above the sharp edge. This will help to buffer the stress on the knife so that it is less likely to break. Firmly strike the back of the knife blade with the end of the baton that you shaved the bark off of. It will begin to shear the wood apart. When there is enough room, fit the wedge stick that you made into the crack and remove your knife. Now, baton the wedge stick into the crack and pry the piece of kindling off.

FUEL

This is the larger wood that will give strength to your fire. The fuel will turn into strong coals that can burn through green and damp wood. These coals will also be the best for cooking and boiling water. To begin with, you will still want fairly dry wood until the coals are established. Divide the fuel into three different piles in the same fashion used for the kindling. The first will be larger than thumb size. Slowly add this in with the last of the kindling. The largest wood in this pile will be about wrist-size.

Work the largest pieces of the first pile into the second. These will be wrist-size and larger. At this point, you should have a decent fire established. When the bigger pieces of this pile are burning well, it will be time to put on some of the heavy fuel. Do not add too much. The fire still needs oxygen and you do not want to smother it. Heavy fuel can be the size of your arm and work its way up to full sized logs if need be.

Once the fire has a nice base of coals, you will not have to be as selective with what you burn. Now it is all right to put in the occasional piece of green or moist wood. Harder woods like ash, maple oak, and elm, will burn longer and give off more heat. Evergreen, alder, willow, and other soft woods will burn rapidly and throw sparks which could be a danger if the fire is situated too close to the shelter. Birch wood will be a preferred choice for fuel. It burns readily but not too fast. In addition to that, you will not need to worry about birch throwing sparks.

The majority of the time you will not need to burn big logs. Logs are better used for shelter construction or building a firewall, which I will explain later in this chapter. If logs are the only thing to work with, then do not waste time and effort processing them. Feed them into the fire slowly and let the flames do the work. Save your energy.

DESIGN

There is a multitude of different ways you can build a fire. Because this guide is focused on simple practicality, I will keep you concentrated on one. The teepee fire is the one that virtually everyone knows and is the best choice almost every time. This design provides ventilation and wind protection while the fire is still small. It concentrates the heat in the center and feeds itself as the outer wood burns away and falls inward.

The tee pee is also easy to prepare in a fashion that will allow you to ignite the tinder with some kindling already in place. With wet ground, it will be built in the exact same way, with the inclusion of the fire platform described above. The teepee fire is also one of the best for burning through the wood that is moist since the drying process begins before the wood falls to the center.

The teepee fire is easy to learn and many of you have probably already done so. The focus should be on incorporating it with the tinder and working through the kindling and fuel stages. Once you have perfected this method, feel free to move on to other fire designs. Know that you will always come back to the teepee because it is simply the most suitable for almost every occasion.

When it is time to cook or boil water on the fire, the pointed shape of the teepee will be burned down, and the fire should have a hot bed of coals. The fire will still require more fuel, but you will need to isolate some of those coals for use. This is best done by placing a couple of flat rocks into the side of the fire pit. The stone will also transfer heat as it is warmed by the coals. Pieces of green or saturated wood can work as well if need be.

An open area between the rocks will have coals fed into it and act like a small stove by concentrating the heat. Use a stick to push the coals into the stove and periodically add more so that the heat is constant. Surround the remainder of the fire with a few big pieces of fuel and continue to feed it with smaller wood. This will keep the fire's core hot and start to slowly burn the larger pieces of fuel which will supply more coals when you need them to continue cooking or bolster the fire after you are done.

LIGHTING

I would like to say that I have mastered the fire, but there is one thing that you must know. Sooner or later, the wilderness will humble you. Even those who are the very best in the world at lighting fires will come across circumstances that add up to failure. Put that bit of knowledge in your back pocket and deal with it. The same thing applies to life in general. You just can't win all the time. At this point, there are only two options. You can give up, which defies the meaning of survival, and to me, that is no option at all. Or, you dissect the problem, eliminate negative factors, integrate solutions, and TRY AGAIN.

I can still vividly remember lighting my first fire by using primitive methods. It was a feeling of elation, an accomplishment over the elements. While I was at war, two of my survival companions were at home investing months of their time into perfecting the art of the bow drill. The bow drill is one of the prehistoric forms of creating fire through friction.

Their learning was reinforced by literature, professional guidance, and many videos of experts who had become proficient at this task. They tested a variety of woods, different measurements, slight changes of angle, and adjustments in pressure. Needless to say, the learning curve was extreme, and the process was painfully wrought with frustration. There was a lot of failure and struggle but in the end, the two of them became exceptional at this skill.

When I came home, it was my turn to give it a try. The hard learning was done. All the blood, sweat, and tears had been shed. Okay, so maybe there wasn't any weeping during the ordeal. The point is that I was fortunate enough to have two superb coaches who could walk me through the process. With their guidance, I spent all of one day finding the proper materials and constructing my bow drill kit. The list of mistakes that I would have made without them is quite lengthy and would have added a few pages to this chapter.

The following day I was ready to begin the process. There were a couple of failures, but with some tweaks to my kit and improvements in technique, I was rewarded with elation as the tinder bundle burst into flame.

I am not going to teach you the bow drill here. Why, you might ask? I know it sounds exciting and fun. Indeed, it is, but the purpose of the story was to prove a point. This is an advanced technique that will require many hours of practice and even then, it is hard to do unless the conditions are right. Besides, most people will not be hauling a bow drill kit with them everywhere.

It is something that normally takes too much time to procure and construct if you need it quickly. Many guides will show this as a means of fire and describe it in a paragraph to a few pages. The truth is that the intricate detail involved in friction fire is something that can have an entire book dedicated to it. I do not want to discourage you from trying the bow drill when the time is right, but this book is about being intelligently prepared.

Let us hope that you took my advice and put a lighter in your pocket before heading out. I promise you will be glad you did. It is a small reliable and cheap solution. There is no reason not to have one handy. With this simple tool, you shouldn't have a problem getting a fire going even when things are quite wet.

I prefer to carry a Bic® lighter. It is durable and will be the most trustworthy. If it gets wet and will not light, do not worry. Turn the wheel with your thumb and blow on it or put it in a dry pocket. It will work again once the moisture is gone. Even after the lighter is dead, you can slowly turn the wheel to make fine particles of flint. After collecting them, you can pile them onto your tinder and get it to burn with a spark from the lighter.

FERROCERIUM

The next thing that I recommend is a ferrocerium rod. It is regularly called a ferro rod or flint and steel. This material was invented by the chemist, Carl Auer von Welsbach, who combined iron and cerium in 1903. This unique material will throw a shower of sparks that burn at about 3,000 °C when rapidly shaved from the rod. It is something that I keep in all my backpacks. They are very long-lasting, cheap to obtain, and lightweight. The robust heat of the sparks works well and is a solid backup to that lighter.

Buy one that has a rod which measures about three or four fingers long. The short ones are much harder to get a strong spark from. I get the ones that have a steel scraping tool with them. Your knife will work but it is not the best treatment for the blade. A small handle is nice, but you should make sure that it is solidly glued in place because they will occasionally come out.

Get some practice using it before tossing it into your pack. Read the instructions. Frequently, the rod will have a black covering that needs to be scraped off before use. Once that is done, get a nice wad of dry tinder and try to ignite it. Different pressure, angle, and speed with the steel scraper will yield different results. It should only take a few minutes before you are able to throw a strong shower of sparks. Get close to the tinder and direct them into the center. When it begins to smolder, gently blow on it until it takes flame. The ferro rod is a great way to practice. It forces you to work for the fire. The lighter is too easy, which is exactly why I want you to have it.

SUN

Another fairly simple way to light a fire is by harnessing the power of the sun with a lens or through reflection. Many of us have childhood memories of burning things with a magnifying glass or perhaps we were introduced to this process in science class. The sun's extreme energy can be refined into a fine point of concentration by using a lens or reflection off a concave surface.

At times, you may already have a lens with you. Removing the lens from a pair of binoculars, monocular, or rifle scope will be the best. It is also possible to use the curved portion of a clear plastic bottle filled with water or the corner of a clear plastic bag that has water in it. The bottom of a clear glass bottle or jar can be used. If you wear glasses that correct farsightedness, they can also work with a drop of water added to the inside curve of the lens. Fire can even be accomplished with the glass from a vehicle headlight or clear ice that is polished into the right shape with your hands.

A biconvex lens will work the best. This means that it is curved outward on both sides, and therefore bends the light twice, for a stronger magnification. Bottle bottoms, eyeglasses, and headlight covers only curve in one direction. Hold the convex side downward and put a droplet of water into the center of the depression. The water will have a rounded form that will make your lens biconvex and yield better results. Ice will need to be shaped into a biconvex form at the correct thickness. This will be harder, and you need to make sure that water does not melt off of it and drop onto the tinder bundle when you use it.

Using the lens will require clear sky and is best when the sun is close to being directly overhead. High sun is a must when using water and a convex surface. Place the tinder bundle that you are lighting next to a tepee of kindling and extra tinder. You will need to get it into the prepared tepee right away and will only have a few seconds to get it all burning. Make sure everything is ready. If you will have to move the tinder bundle from a sunny location to the fire pit, place it on top of some tree bark or some green leaves. This way you can pick it up safely.

Having a flat piece of tinder in the center of the tinder bundle will give you a place to focus the light onto. Thin pieces of birch bark, paper, or torn pieces of dry leaf layered atop one another works well. It is best to focus the beam on something black or dark colored. White will reflect the light and it will be hard to get enough heat. Rub a bit of dirt or coal dust on the tinder if you need to color it. Having a small pile of finely crushed powder from dry bark or coal on top of the flat tinder works very well.

Situate the lens over the tinder and move it up or down to create the smallest point of light that is focused onto the flat piece of tinder. Squint your eyes and try not to stare directly at the point of light. Prop your elbows on the ground so that the beam is stable and stays on the same spot. A good lens, used correctly, will work in about twenty seconds. Otherwise, there can be some trial and error which might take a good deal longer.

Once the tinder begins to smoke, blow on it gently to feed in some oxygen to the heat that you are creating. Place tiny particles of tinder onto the spot that begins to burn. Continue to burn the area with the lens. Dry tinder should puff into flame when it is ready. Get it into the tepee quickly before it burns through. Add in more tinder until the small kindling starts burning.

Reflection is done a bit differently. This will involve a concave surface that will focus the light together and bounce it back outward. Many flashlights will have a reflective piece that focuses the light from the bulb. The same will hold true for some vehicle lights. With the pieces that had a bulb in them, you should be able to poke some dry grass or other tinder into the hole in the center and the sunlight will create enough heat to get it going.

Unfortunately, aluminum cans have begun to litter even remote areas of wilderness. The noncorrosive nature of this metal means that they do not break down and disappear either. Fortunately, we can still use them in a time of need. By polishing the underside of the can with clay or very fine silt you can get a mirror-like shine. If you set this in line with the sun, it will send a beam of light upward. You will need to hold the tinder bundle in that beam and move it until you find the most focused point. This one can be a bit tricky but will work with enough patience.

BATTERY

The stored energy inside a battery can also be a clever way to get a fire going. Use care when working with a larger battery because it can produce a nasty shock or burn. Connecting jumper cables or wires to a vehicle battery and touching the opposite ends of the cables together will create a spark. Though the spark is not as hot as the spark from a ferro rod, this can work.

If you have a pencil, you can use your knife to strip the wood from one side to expose the graphite. Hook one end of the jumper cables to the battery. The other clamps will connect to each end of the pencil piece. Make sure there is surface connection to the graphite. The heat that runs through the graphite will quickly ignite the wood part of the pencil. Use a length of the pencil that is just over the width of two fingers. The other pieces can be used later.

You can also use the compact batteries that you might have in some flashlight or other simple electronics. Connecting conductive material to each end will complete the circuit. There must be a fine point in the middle of the conductor that will become hot faster because more energy is traveling through a small area. This can be done with foil, a gum wrapper, thin wire, or steel wool. Wire is more likely to be something that you could salvage from a vehicle, but the others may be available.

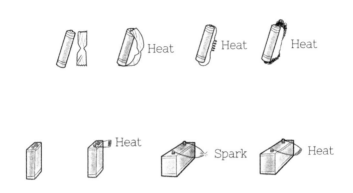

Use gloves or pieces of bark to hold the ends of your conductor in place because they may become hot. A 9-V battery can just be touched to steel wool to get it started. This works nicely even if it is wet. Using foil or a gum wrapper will require a portion cut from the center to make an hourglass shape.

With wire, it is good to separate the strands of wire and make a small coil by wrapping it around a tiny stick. Remove the stick, and you will have a filament where the heat will concentrate. Touching the filament of the conductor to tinder, while still connected to the battery, should get it started. Fine tinder like plant fibers and down from airborne seeds will give better results.

FIREWALL

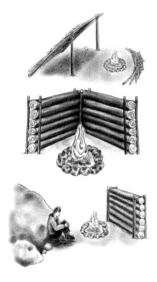

A heat reflector or firewall can greatly increase the benefit of even a gentle blaze when they are used in conjunction. This simple device will protect the fire from the wind, conserve on fuel consumption, increase the heat, force the smoke upward and can be an effective way to dry wood at the same time. A reflector is often used to send warmth toward the shelter area. If directed at a large rock or cliff face, the stone will retain heat much longer and can make the area quite comfortable.

There are a few different ways to construct a firewall and it does not take much time for the comparative value. For a simple wall, space two pairs of waist-high stakes about the span of your arms apart. Drive them into the ground so that wood can be placed horizontally between the stakes. The wall should be one arm's length away from the fire pit. This can also be done with four pairs of stakes to create a wedge-shaped wall.

Often, it will be good to make a simple wall out of wood pieces that you need to dry. Stacking them in a semicircular shape is effective. As the pieces dry out they can be added to the fire and replaced with new ones. This is the practice that I prefer because it suits more functions and can be easily moved to make adjustments for wind changes and the size of the fire.

DIRT TIME

We have barely scratched the surface when it comes to different ways to get a fire started or materials that you can use. These are easy ways to utilize the things which you might have or be able to salvage. Fire-starting is an enjoyable skill to practice and it helps to develop patience through trial and error.

Train your awareness to identify various tinder materials and test them out. Start working with the ferro rod and some different tinder. This will help you to learn more about the tinder and how it ignites. Blend in different accelerants to see how they work. Use what you learn and then apply it to the different lens and battery techniques. You want to be able to get a fire burning in virtually any place or condition.

Remember the importance of having everything that is needed before starting the fire process. Expect to have failures but just keep at it. Failing is a necessary part of growth and should be embraced. Working through it will make you stronger when you need it most. The importance of fire will justify the effort in a multitude of ways.

Become proficient with these techniques and then try some of the more complex methods. The things learned here will better direct you toward success with the more complicated ways to start a fire. I truly do want you to learn friction fire at some point. Eventually, it would be awesome to graduate to a level where you are able to use a knife to gather what you need and start a primitive fire in any condition.

FOOD

"THE INSTINCT TO SURVIVE WILL NEVER CHANGE, NEITHER WILL THE HUMAN BODY'S AMAZING ABILITY TO ENDURE."

—JOHN 'LOFTY' WISEMAN,
SAS SURVIVAL HANDBOOK

Lasting thirty days without food seems completely unreasonable, but it is realistically possible in dire situations. The truth is that it will almost never come to that. Starvation in the wilderness is statistically one of the least likely ways that you could die. Of the few cases where it actually happens, the majority of those who perish from starvation will do so with a virtual buffet of edible things around them. Almost every time, the deciding factor boils down to knowledge.

Our bodies can sustain themselves for a very long time with the food reserves that are stored within the tissues. Refraining from overexertion will prolong this process. On a regular day, it is normal for the body to burn through about two thousand calories. A high rate of activity, extensive movement through the bush or hard work can double or triple that number.

Your body is like a fire. It will consume fuel and convert it into energy. To the body that energy equates to heat, recovery, healing, and movement. If managed intelligently, it will generally only require small amounts of fuel to perform the necessary duties. Just like there are few times that you will earnestly need a roaring fire, gorging yourself with a feast is largely unnecessary. Both are a waste of valuable resources.

If you trace our native ancestors back, it is clear that they predominantly survived by hunting and gathering. They made a way of life out of being opportunistic. Always be watchful. Know where and how to look for food. Take whatever you can when the chance arises. If there is an abundance, preserve and save for the hard days ahead. Do not squander.

ESSENTIAL NUTRIENTS

Simply put, calorie replacement is crucial, but it goes deeper than that. It is not enough to just throw fuel into the body and think that the job is done. There are a few things that go into the equation of nourishment that cannot be left out. In the majority of short-term survival situations, this will not be extremely important but for the long term, it is critical to understand the necessities that sustain life from a nutritional standpoint.

The short list will include water, fats, proteins, carbohydrates, vitamins, and minerals. Without these components, the intricate chain that allows our body to function will begin to break down and introduce a multitude of detrimental problems which are best avoided.

There are numerous accounts of trappers and pioneers who went off into the wilderness with survival skills and equipment but died because they lacked nutritional knowledge. Many were claimed by something called rabbit starvation. They were eating but not giving the body everything it needed. Rabbit starvation occurs when the diet predominantly consists of lean meat such as rabbit and squirrel.

Having fats in our diet is vital. They help to provide energy and also store extra calories that are not immediately needed. They allow the body to regulate temperature. Fats also contribute to proper cellular, nerve, and brain functions. Not only that, we need fats for essential vitamin absorption. Vitamins A, D, E, and K specifically can only be introduced into the system in conjunction with fat.

Without fats, rabbit starvation will cause digestive problems and diarrhea. This turns into a cycle of water and nutrient loss. After the process begins, it can lead to death in a matter of days. If the only thing to consume is lean meat, you are better off drinking only water. Honestly, you should be able to find enough things that will help to supplement these deficiencies.

Proteins are something that our body does not store, and they need to be replaced regularly. Proteins are broken down into twenty essential amino acids, nine of these can only be provided by diet. On a cellular level, we are unable to build and repair tissue without them. Proteins make up the cell structure and the enzymes that help them function. They enable fluid balance and the ability to clot blood. Proteins also convert into antibodies that remove wastes and help to protect us from bacteria and viruses. Where healing and general health are concerned proteins are a huge factor.

The main source of energy for our brain comes from carbohydrates. Without them, we are unable to think properly. In a dire situation the inability to analyze, remember, and make decisions can quickly lead to death. Carbohydrates also release chemicals in our brain that produce a more positive mood. A deficiency can cause depression and impact our will to survive. Carbs fuel the body and nervous system with energy and will often cover the bulk load of your calorie intake. Adequate digestion is also made possible with a regular intake of carbohydrates.

During the fifteenth century, better ships and navigational knowledge led to much exploration and long voyages at sea. With it came a sickness called scurvy, also known as the plague of the seas. These men were afflicted by many horrible symptoms: blackened skin, ulcers, sensory dementia, tooth loss, fatigue and bleeding from the mouth to name a few. The many symptoms made this problem difficult to understand and prevent. Magellan lost more than eighty percent of his crew while crossing the Pacific in 1520.

This plague would persist without public recognition into the 1740s when the British Commodore George Anson led a squadron of ships across the Pacific. Of the two thousand men only seven hundred survived but even then, there was much speculation and the situation was still misunderstood. We now know that a deficiency in vitamin C and B were the largest contributing factors that led to so many deaths over the span of a few hundred years. There are different specific roles that vitamins play for in our body's functions. It is essential for us to get: A, C, D, E, K, and B vitamins so that we can maintain proper health.

Much like vitamins, minerals also contribute to many aspects of our overall health. The list that we need to get regular doses of includes: sodium, iron, potassium, calcium, chloride, magnesium, phosphorus, and a few trace minerals. The big one is sodium which we covered in the water chapter. Iron is a key element in blood production. The strength of our bones and teeth is largely attributed to calcium and phosphorus. Potassium is an electrolyte that works with sodium to regulate fluid balance and maintain blood pressure. It is also necessary for muscle contraction. Magnesium is a highly important component for more than three hundred different reactions in the body.

The main thing that I want to get across here is that there is a strict importance to making sure that you include a variety of things into your food choices. In the wilderness, it is common to come across a couple of things that are plentiful. This is especially true with a limited knowledge base. You can't stop there. Meeting the body's requirements can only be provided through a variance of the things that we put into it. In nature, there is no magical item which will supply everything you need.

For a short period, lacking in these things will not be detrimental to your health but when days turn into weeks, all of these small things begin to add up and the body will deteriorate into a condition where survival is no longer plausible. In the plant, insect, and animal sections that follow I will highlight some sources where you can obtain the essential nutrients.

FORAGING

This is the art of finding what you need to replenish and meet the demands of your body. The untrained eye may glance about the landscape and believe that there is very little in the way of nourishment. Don't fool yourself. We also stare blankly into a refrigerator full of food and think there is nothing to eat! It is the same thing except that in the wilderness we just need to adjust our perspective.

There are very few places that are completely barren, and chances are that you will not find yourself stuck in them. The world that we live on is teaming with life. This is largely attributed to the energy from the sun, nutrients in the soil and sustainable water. If there is life in the landscape, you should be able to survive there.

As in many of life's tasks, it is foremost to be persistent. This is a numbers game and you always need to be actively observant. There is far more food than you will initially believe. One day, I was having a discussion with one of my survival companions about our ability to locate substantial food sources. It was the dead of winter and we both were having doubts about how well we would do. We were struggling to come up with very many things that we would be able to eat, so we grabbed an edible plant guide and headed to the woods to test the theory.

Once we got there it was a simple process to methodically wander the forest and meadows foraging for something we could use. It was surprising how many things we began to find once we were actively engaged. There were plenty of trees that had something to offer. Under the snow were fallen nuts and varieties of plants that somehow managed to stay fresh and green. Breaking apart rotten logs and turning rocks revealed plenty of insect life that was still active or lying dormant.

On the edge of the woods, there were dry concord grapes and rosehips. This is also where we found the most animal activity. With the snow, tracks were abundant and easy to follow right to the burrows and feeding grounds. We both agreed that trapping would be easier with such clear signs. The meadows were filled with dry plant stalks that held edible seeds or showed us where to find roots and tubers. After a few hours, our doubts were squelched, and we walked away confidently reassured that we would have plenty.

Remember that foraging is a constant part of the everyday activity. Incorporate this into the process when traveling, gathering shelter materials, picking up things for the fire and searching for water. They all have their priorities but in many ways these activities and the acquisition of conscious observation overlap. Watch for the signs and indicators. Know that your food sources need the water just like you do. Understand the habits of the things that you can use for food: where they grow, what they eat, the places they live, when they are active and how they survive. These small bits of knowledge will increase your rate of success and give you a deeper appreciation for the things that can provide for you.

PLANTS

Some kind of vegetation can be found in almost every climate zone. This will often be your most dependable food source. It will also require the least effort to gather and therefore save on energy expenditure. Eating plants will help replenish vitamins, minerals, carbohydrates, fiber, proteins and sometimes even fats. Plants are normally easy to digest and will require less water to do so.

About half of the plant species in the world have at least one portion that is edible. Make sure that you have an understanding of the edible plants in your area and make a positive identification before eating them. Also, know that anything listed as edible can have a reaction with your particular body if it is something that you have never tried before. When there is any doubt whatsoever, you must use the universal edibility test.

Before conducting the test, there a few things to know. First, make sure that there is enough of that plant in your area to make it worth your time. A few handfuls of something does not justify the risk. Understand that there is no safe testing method for fungus. Avoid plants with milky sap unless positively identified as being safe such as dandelion and coconut.

Do not take plant parts that are diseased, wilted, or old. In some cases, these will have harmful molds or develop toxins. Plants with fine hairs, spines, and barbs will cause irritation unless dealt with properly. Be cautious of red or brightly colored plants unless positively identified. Not all parts of the plant may be edible. Separate them into the different parts: leaves, root, stem, flower, seeds, and fruit. When testing, only do so with one person in the group to minimize harmful effects if there are any.

Know that there two main poisons found in plants and both can be easily identified when you are aware of them. Oxalic acid can be distinguished by a sharp stinging, burning, or dry sensation when touched to the tongue or underside of the wrist. Hydrocyanic or prussic acid is recognizable by a smell or taste of bitter almond or sometimes peach. Stay away from anything that falls into these descriptions.

I know that going through all of these steps is lengthy and will take the better part of a day to complete, but it is worth investing that time into finding something that you can utilize every day after that.

THE UNIVERSAL EDIBILITY TEST

1. Select one plant part that will be tested.

2. Crush a portion of the plant and smell for strong acidic or almond-like odors.

3. Abstain from eating for at least eight hours before the eating portion of test. During this time, you may perform the contact portions of the test.

4. Crush a portion of the plant and rub it on the underside of your wrist. Wait fifteen minutes and observe the area for any signs of reaction. If there are any negative signs then, it should be discarded.

5. Hold a portion of the plant on the outside of your lip for three minutes and check for burning or itching sensation.

6. Hold a portion of the plant on the corner of your mouth for three minutes and check for burning or itching sensation.

7. Hold a portion of the plant on the tip of your tongue for fifteen minutes and check for burning or itching sensation.

8. Hold a portion of the plant under your tongue for fifteen minutes and check for burning or itching sensation.

9. Chew a portion of the plant and hold it in your mouth for fifteen minutes and check for burning or itching sensation. Do not swallow any of it.

10. If during all of the contact portions of the test there was no indication of: burning, itching, discomfort, stinging, numbness, swelling, throat soreness or unpleasant reaction, you may then proceed to ingest a small portion of the plant.

11. Wait for eight hours and do not eat or drink anything else. Be aware of signs that may include: swelling or soreness in the mouth, bloating, repeated belching, pain in the stomach or abdominal area, and nausea. If there are any adverse effects, drink plenty of water. If the symptoms are severe, induce vomiting and follow with plenty of water.

12. If there are no ill effects, then eat a small handful of the plant and wait for eight hours.

13. Once at this stage, the plant portion can be considered safe if you have not encountered any negative signs or effects.

Note: All individual parts of the plant must be tested separately. Just because one portion of the plant has proven to be safe does not mean that the entire plant is safe. Also, know that cooking a portion of the plant can change the results of the test by getting rid of harmful toxins.

Eating a good selection of different plants can provide almost everything that your body needs. Often their abundance can make plants something that we easily overlook. It is not uncommon for the survivor to walk all day upon a feast, ready for the taking.

Ninety-nine percent of grasses are edible. They are found almost everywhere and range from wheats, oats, and meadow grasses all the way up to the giant varieties like bamboo. Eat the small and tender shoots or the white portion at the base when it is pulled from the plant. Pieces that are tough and fibrous can be chewed for the juices which are full of vitamins. Spit out anything that is hard to chew as it will be difficult to digest. The best part will be the seed heads and small grains. These can be eaten raw, gathered to make flour and millet, or added into soups. Grasses and their seeds will be a rich source of carbohydrates, vitamins, protein, and trace fats.

Larger seeds and especially nuts are a great way to replenish protein and fat. Frequently overlooked by humans, oak trees drop many acorns that are a prized food source for animals in the autumn and winter. Numerous species of oak grow throughout the world. Shell the gathered acorns and crush them into a pulp.

Boiling the pulp in one or two changes of water will remove the bitter tannins and make them more palatable. The pulp can then be strained with some cloth and immediately eaten or dried for later use. One large oak can easily drop enough to fill your belly and sustain future meals. Acorns, seeds, and other nuts are long-lasting and can be carried until you need to eat them.

Another plant that is regularly passed by on the search for food is the humble pine or evergreen. Sure, they are a great choice for shelter materials, but many would believe they are of little value as a food source. Wrong. In the springtime, the male trees produce protein-rich pollen anthers that can be eaten. Every species will bear cones that contain seeds or pine nuts which can be gathered in the fall and early winter. Although most are small and take time to collect, they are a favorite of squirrels and many birds for good reason.

During the entire year, pines will have needles that are a valuable place to get that much-needed Vitamin C. The new needles in the spring are tender enough to eat right off the tree. Chew the mature needles for the juices or cut and boil them to make spruce tea. The soft inner bark of the young branches can also be taken year-round and is surprisingly nourishing. The porcupine is known to survive by feasting on this bark throughout most of the winter months.

Be sure to avoid the Ponderosa Pine, Yew, and Norfolk Island Pine which are the three species that are poisonous. Learn to identify these three and you will be able to gather plenty of food from all the others.

The above plants are just a few, but they can be found in most locales. To go into all the plants that can be eaten would be vastly extensive and overwhelming for this guide. I have dozens of books that expound upon edible plants, and we haven't even brought up the medicinal and healing properties that they provide as well.

The subject is better focused upon exclusively and in a more concentrated degree. Don't think for a second that because I haven't fully covered this topic that it is of small importance. Do yourself a favor and get a plant guide that corresponds with your area. Plants are vastly beneficial, and you cannot afford to overlook what they can provide for you in a time of need.

INSECTS

Bugs! For many of us in the Western world, this suggestion sparks sudden distaste. Put that prejudiced notion aside. The truth is that over two billion people worldwide include insects as part of their regular diet. For primitive humans, these easy-to-catch morsels were an abundant food staple. Surprisingly, many of them are fortified with more nutrients than fish or meat. Insects are found almost everywhere and constitute the largest supply of protein on Earth. Hunting or trapping them is easy to do and will almost always yield results even for the unskilled.

Remember that it is never smart to pass on a meal of any kind in a survival situation. Your body begins to cannibalize itself in a matter of days when nutrients are not replaced. Every bit of depletion means that your odds of making it are lessened. Get over the disgust and picture yourself living to indulge in your favorite meal again.

The greater majority of insects are edible but there are a few indicators that will tell you which ones to steer clear of. Those with bright or distinct colors that stand out are often marked that way to show predators that they are poisonous. Pungent smells are also used as a deterrent and should be heeded as such. The ones that have hairy bodies or spines will often cause irritation and are better left alone. Stinging insects and any that inflict a harmful bite are also not the best choices.

You should also always avoid the ones that are known to carry diseases such as flies, ticks, and mosquitoes. Naturally, there are exceptions to these rules. Oddly enough, stink bugs can be boiled to get rid of the stench, hairy tarantulas are regularly eaten in parts of South America, and scorpions are widely favored for their crab-like taste once the poisonous stinger is removed.

Honestly, you should be able to find enough bugs that do not pose any risk. When there is any danger that it could be harmful, or you are in the least bit uncertain, it is best to find something else. If you are concerned that they may have been feeding on something poisonous, it is preferred to purge them first. Keep your catch in a container for a day with some plants that are safe to eat. This should be enough time to get anything bad through their system.

One day in the army when we were training in the field, I caught a huge locust that was bigger than my thumb. Soldiers have a knack for coming up with silly ideas to overcome boredom. One of the guys dared me to eat it for ten dollars. Cleverly, I began to play on some common fears and the disgust factor that troubles many people when it comes to eating bugs. Before long, money was being passed around and the whole platoon was involved. So, I made a good show of it. With wings spread and kicking legs, I chewed it up and down it went. Inevitably, I survived the ordeal and was able to walk away with a week's pay in my pocket.

While I may have made it through my raw locust-eating escapade unscathed, understand that a lot of insects will carry parasites or bacteria, so it is always best to cook them before eating. First, remove hard legs, wings, shells and the head. Boiling works well for small things like ants, but it is more common to roast larger morsels over the fire on a stick or in your metal container. Roasting is also going to be a more pleasurable way of eating them as it will often enhance the flavor. If you are still struggling with the thought of ingesting these critters, try to crush them and add the pieces into a soup mixed with some plants.

Grasshoppers and crickets are a good choice. With the exception of cold wintertime, they can be found throughout the year in most places. Grasshoppers frequent sunny prairies and grasslands. Catch them in the mornings or before dark when the cooler air slows them down. Crickets like cooler places that are more shaded because they are predominantly nocturnal. Find them hiding under logs and rocks during the day. Catch them in small pit traps or bottle traps at night. These traps work well and will capture many insects. Crickets and grasshoppers are best when roasted over the fire and are commonly eaten in many parts of the world. Because of their size, they can prove to be great sources of nourishment.

Ants and termites may be small, but their colonies often harbor a large number that is consolidated in one place. Termites are more common in warm environments and can be located by their obvious mounds which also make good fire starter when broken apart. Submerging pieces of their mound will force them out into the water where they can be collected. Use caution since some of them have pincers for biting. Ants are found everywhere but you will want to stay well away from the dangerous varieties such as fire ants and bullet ants which can inflict serious pain and allergic reaction.

Ants also contain formic acid which can be considered unpleasant to the taste, but this will be depleted through boiling. Watch for their mounds or sometimes they can be found under rocks and living in dead logs. Also, following a column of ants back to the colony can work. Digging into their home will make them come out. Poke a small stick into the center of the pile and they can be plucked off when they climb up. Don't forget to gather the eggs and larvae which can contain more nutrients than the adults. The adults will try to move them to a safe location when the mound is disturbed, and you can easily take them at this time.

Earthworms and grubs/beetle larvae may not make the list for being highly appetizing, but they will do a great job of supplementing proteins and much-needed fats. Beetle larvae are most efficient at turning the cellulose from trees into digestible fats which is something we are unable to do. These will also be a good source of minerals such as iron. I have eaten some questionable things, but this group is even hard for me to stomach.

Worms and grubs are easily found by digging in the ground,

breaking apart rotten logs and turning over rocks. Some of them can even be found in the winter. Boil, roast or add them to soups. Earthworms can even be dried in the sun for later use.

The greater majority of beetles themselves are also safe to eat. Almost fifteen hundred species worldwide have been confirmed as safe. A common food selection in many parts of the world, most of them are larger in size and contain a lot of nutrients. Those which have toxins should be edible after boiling but it is best to avoid species of blister beetle, bombardier beetles, and choresine beetles. Beetles are regularly found roaming the ground, on plants they are eating or hiding beneath things in shaded areas. They are most commonly roasted before eating.

Woodlice, sow bugs, roly-polies, potato bugs, etc. are all the same but have many names because they are all of a highly adaptable species from which there are over five thousand varieties found worldwide. Actually, they are the only prehistoric species of crustacean that has evolved to survive on land. The few places that they are not found are polar regions and those with almost no moisture.

They can be easily collected in large numbers underneath rocks, logs, and leaf litter. Boiled or roasted, they will have a flavor that is likened to shrimp. Because of their close relation, you should steer clear if you are allergic to shellfish. For those who enjoy seafood, this could be a surprising treat.

ANIMAL

The major classifications of vertebrae are mammals, birds, reptiles, fish, and amphibians. I will also include invertebrates such as mollusks and crustaceans. Bear in mind that while these will adhere more closely with our general idea of food, the animal group will often require additional energy expenditure, time, effort, failure, and risk. While we ideally picture ourselves pulling juicy fish from the river or roasting choice meat over a spit on the fire, that is seldom the reality of the situation.

Holding on to this mindset will surely mean that you will also learn how to cope with hunger. Larger game is far trickier to catch, capable of defending itself and less plentiful. They are always alert to the danger and have acuter senses than ours. Of course, we never want to pass on a good meal and given the proper knowledge, you might get the perfect opportunity. There are some helpful tricks that I will talk about in the next chapter which can be utilized to bring in some more substantial food.

MOLLUSKS

This is a large group that includes over fifty thousand species: clams, mussels, oysters, cockles, scallop, winkles, snails, whelk, octopus, and squid. Each of these commonly recognized names has many species. They are found in or near saltwater, freshwater, and sometimes on land. Many of them can be eaten but with so many species involved, there are naturally going to be some that are poisonous or pose risk.

Many of them are filter feeders and if the water that they live in is polluted, they can be known to store chemicals and toxins in their bodies. There are varieties of cone snail that can produce a hypodermic needle-like barb which is used to inject poison that can be very painful or even fatal. The tiny blue-ring octopus has a bite that almost always results in paralysis that is followed by death. Even the land snails that are safe to eat can hold toxins from the things they eat and should be purged for a few days.

While many mollusks can be easy to find and collect, be very sure that they have been positively identified and even then, use caution. Without proper cooking to get rid of bacteria they can still make you quite sick. When there is any doubt, just leave them alone or use them as bait to catch something that is safer to eat.

CRUSTACEANS

With their hard shells and jointed extremities, they are easily recognizable. Most of us are familiar with lobster, crabs, prawns, and crayfish. Boiled, steamed or roasted, all of them are safe to eat except a few varieties in Australia with black tipped claws. Overall, they are low in fat content but are high in protein and will provide some needed vitamins and minerals.

Most of them live in saltwater but crayfish are found in many lakes and streams. Freshwater prawns are more common in temperate and tropical regions. Find crabs along shorelines, amidst rocks, or burrowed into the sand. Most shrimp, lobster, and larger crabs will more likely be in deeper water which will make them harder to catch. Crayfish and freshwater prawns will roam many different areas of the places they live but often stay near shallower water.

Crustaceans can be caught by hand but many of them have spines and claws that can be rather powerful and cause injury. It is best to wear leather gloves. You will find that they are able to jet through the water when trying to flee, making them hard to catch. Those on land can sometimes be stunned by swatting them with a leafy branch or throwing a handful of small stones and sand. Most crustaceans are more active at night when they are feeding.

Because they are scavenging predators it will normally be easiest to catch them with bait and bottle traps that they can fall into and not escape from. Sometimes spears or branches fashioned into nets can be used to obtain those in deeper water. For the freshwater varieties, catching by hand, with a dip net or herding them into a larger net that is stretched across a stream is recommended. There is a learning curve that comes with catching the different varieties, but the tasty meal will be well worth it. Try different things and remember to manipulate their scavenging nature.

AMPHIBIANS

Their classification comes from the Greek word amphibios, which means to live a double life. The eggs are laid in the water. They hatch with lungs that allow them to breathe in an aquatic habitat. As these cold-blooded vertebrates mature, they will begin to transform and develop lungs that are able to breathe out of the water. After this metamorphosis, most of them spend their lives on land near moist environments, but they will always return to the water to lay their eggs. The most common are frogs, toads, newts, and salamanders but also includes caecilians which are limbless and serpentine.

Frogs are eaten in many parts of the world and there is a wide variety that are considered safe to eat. The most common are the European green frog, American bullfrog, and East Asian bullfrog. Understand that all frogs release some kind of toxin from their skin as a defense mechanism. It is often hard to determine which ones are harmful. Even when properly identified, the skin will need to be removed before cooking.

Many of the highly poisonous species live in the tropics and warmer climates. Many of these are identified by vibrant colors and patterns but this is not foolproof. The right frogs can be a viable food source, but the wrong ones can make you seriously ill or kill you outright. Use caution.

Most of the time you will find them near shallow places by the shores of lakes and streams. Frogs are predators that largely feed on insects, but some larger species will also eat small animals. They can be caught by hand, but it is better to cover them with a shirt or leafy branch, so they do not escape as easily.

To skin them you will need to cut a slit in the skin across the back from one front leg over to the other. Push a finger under the skin and pull it down to the ankles of the back legs. Cut off all the feet and head to pull the skin free. Removing the legs will give you the largest portions of meat. The remainder is best used as bait for traps. Make sure to wash your hands and the meat very well with drinking water. The frog meat is best roasted over the fire, but boiling is fine as well. Overall, this is just a good source of protein and some trace minerals.

Toads will have a skin that is drier and bumpy. You will also see a conspicuous swollen gland behind their eyes. Their short stumpy legs are less adapted for swimming because they prefer areas that are a bit dryer. All species of toads are poisonous except one, so it is best to leave them alone. Most animals avoid them as well and generally speaking they do not make suitable bait either.

The largest amphibian is the giant salamander, which has been known to survive to be well over a hundred years old and can grow to be more than one hundred pounds and nearly six feet long. These docile creatures are endangered and heavily protected. The few species are only found in remote regions of China, Japan, and North America. In places, poachers do take them as an illegal food source but even in an emergency, you should not.

All smaller varieties of newts and salamander secrete toxins from their skin. In most cases, they are better off not handled. Touching your face or eyes afterward could cause serious irritation. Some of them can even produce piercing barbs from their sides that are able to deliver venom. Because most of them are quite small, the limited sustenance is not worth the risk of poisoning. Pollution and loss of habitat have also greatly decreased their populations so if you should come across them, take a moment to appreciate their existence and find something better to eat.

REPTILES

The different order of reptiles will include alligators and crocodile, turtles, snakes, and lizards as well as the unique tuatara of New Zealand. All of them are cold-blooded vertebrates which are covered with dry scales or hard protective plates and spines. The majority of reptiles lay eggs but there are a few that will birth live young. Most of them are carnivores, although a few are known to eat only plants.

There should not be an issue with eating reptile eggs, providing that they are thoroughly cooked. Boil or fry them but do not be surprised if you find a developing animal inside. Just make it part of the meal. In many cultures, people eat the eggs of turtles, snakes, iguana, and even crocodile or alligator. Unfortunately, the popularity of consuming turtle eggs has severely diminished or endangered turtle populations. Only take turtle eggs as a last resort and even then, only take a few before covering the nest and returning it to its normal state.

Lizards range in size from the those which are almost the size of a person, to some that are smaller than your little finger. There are only three lizards that are known to be poisonous. Komodo dragons are huge and dangerous but only live on four small islands of Indonesia. In the remote chance that you find yourself on one of these islands, you will surely be warned to avoid them at all cost. It is likely that if you saw one of these six-foot beasts, with long claws and bacteria-ridden saliva dripping from its sharp teeth, you would want nothing to do with it.

The Gila monster of the southwestern United States and the

Mexican state of Sonora is another one to watch out for. They are typically the size of your forearm and recognized by their distinct speckled and striped pattern. It is usually a cream, yellow, or orange color on a dark grey or black body. The skin has a beaded texture and they have a flat body with a broad head and tail. If you are in their habitat, be careful when moving stones because they like to hide underneath them.

A slightly larger cousin to the Gila monster is the Mexican beaded lizard. The two species are principally found in Mexico and southern Guatemala. They share the same visual features as their cousin, but the beaded skin tends to have more of the cream color and less orange.

The bite from any of these lizards will produce severe pain, swelling, and anaphylactic shock. In a survival situation, without proper medical care, this can easily lead to death. Although the meat from these lizards is edible, you will have to decide if obtaining it is worth the risk. Before cleaning the body, remove the head and bury it to prevent poisoning.

Aside from these distinct few, all other lizards are nonpoisonous. Lizards are abundant in tropical and subtropical regions but surprisingly live in many places that have cold winters as well. Most prefer sunny places but can be found almost anywhere when they are hunting for food. A great number of them are good climbers, so look high and low when hunting lizards.

They normally have a timid nature and will try to run from you at astonishing speeds. A few larger varieties, such as the monitor and iguana are known to be aggressive and will bite or lash you with their tails. Use a club and wear gloves. Anything with a mouth that is big enough to clamp down on your finger will try to do just that and should be handled with care.

Lizards will be slower in the morning hours before their body has a chance to warm up. As a young boy, I lived in a tropical region and spent many days in pursuit of these reptiles. Patience and persistence will yield results. Swat smaller ones with a branch or sometimes they will fall into a pit trap.

It is not uncommon for lizards to have bacteria and parasites on their bodies, so be sure to wash your hands after handling them and cook the meat fully. Skin and remove the entrails from large ones, then roast or boil the meat. Roast small ones over the fire by impaling them through the mouth with a stick. When the skin bubbles and cracks apart, the meat is done. The meat will replenish protein, minerals, and small amounts of fat.

Snakes are found almost everywhere except in arctic regions. All snakes are carnivores and need to regularly hunt for prey. Several species spend much of their time in and around lakes or wetlands. Some will take to the trees, but most can be found on the ground basking in sunny places or hiding under rocks and logs. Their cold blood will cause them to move more slowly in the morning or before dark. In places with cold winter, they will hibernate.

All non-poisonous and poisonous snakes that live on land or in freshwater are a potential food source. It is widely known that some snakes have a bite that is extremely dangerous. Always use caution when dealing with snakes, even if you believe that it is not poisonous. It is not worth the risk. If your area is known to have deadly snakes, learn to recognize them. Also, be slow, methodical, and cautious when hunting because their camouflage can be astounding.

All snakes should be handled in the same manner. Identified or not—you will be smart to regard all snakes as though they are venomous. Some can closely resemble others or change appearances at different stages of their life. You want to be safely fed, not agonized and dead.

Use a long stick or spear to hold down the body close to the head. Stay well away when doing this as some will be able to rapidly lash out and try to bite. When the snake's body is secured, use another stick or a rock to bash them over the head until you are very sure that it is dead. Even then, you will not want to stop holding the body because some snakes can fake death quite convincingly.

Take the second stick or rock and pin down the body just behind the head. Hold it firmly in place and use your knife to cut off the head. Reflexes can cause a poisonous snake's head to inject venom even after it is removed. It needs to be buried for safety. If you are not sure, bury it anyway

To clean the snake, you will cut a slit lengthwise along the underside of the skin. Remove the innards for later use as bait and peel the skin from the body. After washing it, the meat can be roasted over the fire or boiled. The meat should pull free of the ribs when it is done. Take care not to swallow the small bones. Snake is a good source of protein, trace minerals, and some fat.

In years past, eating turtle meat was more prevalent, but there are still many places throughout the world where it is still common. Undergoing few changes since prehistoric times, these animals are highly adapted survivors that can be found almost everywhere. Sadly, due to overhunting, loss of habitat and pollution, over sixty percent of the turtle and tortoise species are listed as vulnerable or endangered. Just as mentioned earlier with the turtle eggs, because they are facing extinction I implore you to choose a different meal unless the circumstances are dire.

If the situation absolutely deems necessary, the fat reserves in a turtle are very rich and could be a highly important life saver. Most turtles are carnivores that spend their time in or near water. Tortoises, conversely, will be found on land and are dominantly herbivores. These animals do retreat into their shells as a protection mechanism but be aware that many will try to bite or use their claws when handled. Varieties of snapping turtle can be especially dangerous.

Dating back to prehistoric times, alligators and crocodiles, have been inhabitants of tropical and subtropical climates for a great many years. These intimidating predators grow to be the largest reptiles on Earth and understandably so, reside at the top of the food chain. They are stealthy in the water, astonishingly fast on land and packed with powerful muscle.

In the swamp phase of ranger school, we were instructed on handling poisonous snakes and the American alligator. Identifying the danger and staying clear of it was always the safest bet for us and I will give the same instruction to you. Even the small adolescent ones can inflict terrible damage with their bite. Often, these animals will try to escape but when attacked, they will fight back with a lashing tail or a charge that is led by snapping jaws. There is a reason that they have survived so long. They are dangerous and not to be underestimated.

Yes, if you feel that it is necessary and are ready for a fight, there is good meat under that tough skin. It is fortified with an abundance of fat if you are facing a threatening deficiency. You can find them lurking in the waters, lounging on the banks or stalking through dense vegetation. Attacks on humans are uncommon, but it's important to use your awareness when traversing these places or they may just find you first.

Killing a larger alligator or crocodile is not an easy process and should not be attempted due to the inherent risk. Smaller ones can be bludgeoned with a club to the head. Sometimes a noose or a net can be used to entangle them first. When it is motionless, use the club to hold down the jaws and drive your knife into the place where the spine connects to the base of the skull. It will be hard to know that it is truly dead since the nerves will cause the muscles to twitch long after. I had the pleasure of cleaning a gator when I lived in Florida. Hours after the animal was killed and the meat was cut free of the body, it continued to twitch in my hands. It was a bit unsettling.

When cleaning alligator or crocodile, be prepared to get a dull knife. The hide is tough and will wear down the edge on your blade. The bulk meat will be found in the tail, legs, and neck. Chop off the feet and skin the legs and tail before removing them from the carcass for cooking. Now, cut away the pieces of meat around the neck and the sides of the jaw. There will still be a lot of meat remaining, but you will need to work for it.

Cook it over the fire or boil it to get a fatty broth as well. Gator meat is delicious but without the proper seasonings, the meat will likely have a muddy flavor from the fat. What it lacks in taste will be made up for with protein, fat, and minerals.

BIRDS

When you have the opportunity to catch them, birds are always a safe bet. All birds and their eggs can be eaten. Most have a regular dependency on fresh water and can be found just about anywhere that has a place for them to drink. With the numerous types of birds also comes a variety of places they can be habitually found.

Some will stick to the trees, there are those who feed primarily on the ground, and others tend to be more aquatic. Shorebirds can be found combing the beaches or nesting along rocky seasides. Birds of the wetlands normally feed in the shallows or fish in open water and can be found nesting in the reeds and long marsh grasses.

Aside from the nocturnal predators such as owls, most birds do not see well in the darkness and will take shelter for the night. Smaller birds feel safer in confined places like bushes and thick trees that are hard for larger animals to get into. Many of the bigger ground-feeding birds will roost together in the branches of trees. Wetland birds hunker down in the reeds or adjacent prairies. Shorebirds seek shelter in the rocks or beach grasses.

Following these different movements and learning about their common activities will give you far better chances when hunting. Shortly before darkness and early predawn hours can be good times. Many birds can be baited and either snared or hit with a throwing stick when they get close. Larger birds, especially those which flock together, can be taken with a throwing stick or entangled with some bolas. Floating a bottle or buoy with snares attached will sometimes snag curious waterfowl as well.

Frequently, roosting trees can be identified by morning chatter or many droppings on the ground below. Tie snares in the branches of these trees. Baited spring snares will also work for many bird types. During the autumn, many ducks, geese, and game birds will molt feathers. This will limit their flying capabilities and leave them vulnerable. Also, remember that migration times bring a multitude of birds together into regular places, which can increase your success rate.

Raiding eggs from nests can seem like an easy food source but be advised that it is not uncommon for the parents to be viciously protective. If you leave one egg in the nest and do not make too much of a disturbance, the mother will often lay more eggs and you can return to it several times. It may not be appetizing, but even the contents of mostly developed eggs can be eaten. In the Philippines, people eat a delicacy called Balut. Cooked duck eggs are served with a hatchling that is almost ready to come out of the shell.

Once you have your bird, it will need to be plucked. Plucking will take some time and patience. If you scald the body in hot water, the process can be easier while it is still warm. Dry pluck-ing is often a cleaner way to do it. Start with the large tail and wing feathers and progress to the smaller ones. Remember that feathers can be used for many things like warm insulation, fire starter, fishing lures and arrow flights. When this is done, cut off the head and feet before gutting the bird.

The washed meat can be roasted or boiled with the skin on. It can be done whole or separated into pieces. Larger birds should be separated when roasting over the fire so that the meat cooks evenly through. Any eggs that you procure can be boiled before eating. The shells contain valuable calcium and you will want to thoroughly chew them for consumption as well. Eggs are a great source of protein, B vitamins, vitamin D, some fat, and trace minerals. The meat itself will have protein, some vitamins, and minerals as well as the fat that is primarily concentrated in the skin.

FISH

Most bodies of water have a chance to contain fish. It may be minnows in a tiny stream, panfish in a lake, or an ocean filled with endless bounty. The problem is that unless disaster struck while on a fishing trip, we most likely will not have a pole and tackle box. Fortunately, the methods of catching are as varied as the fish that you will encounter. Understandably, there is vast knowledge that is pertinent to this topic. Later, I will share some common tips, tricks, and methods, but you need to know that successfully catching fish involves a learning process.

All freshwater fish are edible. There is no failsafe way to pick out poisonous ocean fish other than to know them specifically. Just avoid anything that does not look like a typical scaled fish. Skin that is smooth, bumpy, spiny, rough, or bristled will be something to watch out for. Some fish that have toxic flesh are the cowfish, porcupine, stonefish, puffer, and thorn fish.

Most of the poisonous fish live around coral reefs and rocky shores. The predatory fish that feed on them also pose some risk, so stay away from barracuda and big reef fish. The toxin ciguatera is built up in the flesh of the fish and especially the liver. This poisoning is hard to treat without medical attention and dehydration will occur due to the symptoms, so hydration is a must if you believe that you are affected.

Symptoms include numbness and tingling in the mouth, throat, and extremities, weakness, joint and muscle pain, nausea, vomiting, abdominal pain, and diarrhea, headache, fainting, and hives. Stick to small portions of medium-sized fish with a standard appearance and you should be fine. Cooking will not get rid of these toxins, so when there is any doubt, play it safe.

If your catch does not extend past your four fingers when the fish is laid across them, you are in luck, it does not have to be cleaned and can be eaten after cooking (just think sardine). Chew up everything to get the maximum nutrient value. If you managed to get something bigger, it will need to be cleaned. Cut under the throat and remove the gills. Now, make a slit from the anus to the throat. Remove the offal to be used later for bait or trapping. The fish can then be scaled by firmly holding the tail and scraping the blade of your knife toward the head.

Freshwater fish without scales are normally skinned, but this is sometimes difficult and not fully necessary. Just make a few lengthwise cuts in the skin to help it cook more evenly. In a survival situation, the skin and even the eyes should be eaten to get the fats and nutrients that are stored there.

When cooking over the fire, poke a stick through the base of the tail and along the inside of the body to come out through the head. Be sure that it is secure and will not fall off. It is best to cut the fish into portions if you decide to boil it. The meat will flake apart when it is done cooking.

Adding fish to your diet can be very helpful. Aside from protein, most will also have fair amounts of much-needed fat. Fish also contain vitamin D, vitamin A, and B vitamins. This food source will supply many of the vital minerals as well. When fish can be found in proximity to your location, it is definitely worth attempting some methods of catching them which are outlined in the next chapter.

MAMMALS

A plethora of mammal species can be found ranging around the globe. The size of these warm-blooded vertebrae stretches from the tiny mouse to the great blue whale. As a whole, mammals can be safely eaten. Almost all mammals can defend themselves with a bite, claws, or some kind of specialized defense. There are a select few that are venomous and should be left alone but you will rarely encounter them. The pointy nosed little shrew, platypus, European mole, slow loris, and vampire bat will just about complete the list.

From the polar regions, deciduous forests, deserts, tropics, and our oceans, mammals have adapted to live in virtually every known environment. With so many species to be encountered, mammals can be a substantial food source, but be aware that some of them might look at you with those same hungry eyes. Others will only hunger for vegetation, but they can be just as dangerous as the predators that they need to defend themselves from. Horns and hooves are recognizably formidable but do not underestimate the strength and power of even a small animal when it is trying to protect itself.

I would predominantly recommend that you concentrate your focus on smaller game. Look to animals that will provide a single meal or two at the most. First of all, small game comes in more concentrated numbers which will increase your odds. It will also lower your risk of being injured by the animal. This reasoning also alleviates the inherent problems with preservation, storage, and keeping that food from drawing the attention of other hungry animals. There is almost always enough food to survive quite well using this practice.

When there are numerous people to feed, the demand may be different. In this situation, the opportunity to take larger game might be logical. It is also easier to manage the hunting of large animals when there are a few people involved but there is still an elevated risk. Keep in mind that a few people can also be fed by catching smaller game through concentrated effort. Your success rate will still be higher than taking the gamble of spending a lot of time and effort on one big meal.

Because of the range in habitat and size, hunting mammals can vary greatly. Mice can be caught with a buried bottle trap that has a flat rock supported just over the surface to prevent them from jumping out. They will fall in when seeking shelter under the rock or jump in to get at bait placed in the bottom. A two-liter bottle works well for this.

Snares are a good choice for catching medium-sized mammals that are fast and difficult to hunt with improvised weapons. A snare must be made with strong cordage so that the animal does not break free when struggling against it. Use these for rodents like rabbit, squirrel, and raccoon but don't count out the chances to succeed in catching things such as monkey, coyote and fox. Effective use of snares requires the correct materials and can be tricky to get right. Setting numerous snares and checking them regularly will improve your odds.

At times an improvised weapon can be more prudent. This may be a ranged weapon such as a throwing stick, bolas, or stone. Occasionally, a striking weapon like a club or cudgel will be needed. A good spear will give you the choice to throw it for distance or use it up close when striking or impaling. The particular game and environment will have a strong bearing on your choice of weapon. Sometimes a combination of these will be more effective but remember that making an assortment of weapons also involves added encumbrance.

Preparing mammals for cooking will generally mean that you need to gut and skin them. To gut the animal, cut around the anus and make an incision upward through the skin under the belly up to the rib cage. It is easier to make a small incision so that you can lift the skin and cut outward through the hide. Cutting through the animal's hair is difficult and will rapidly dull your blade. Now, extend the cut from the anus down the inside of both hind legs to make a larger opening.

At this point, you will need to carefully cut open the abdominal area so that you can remove the stomach, bladder, and intestines. Take care so that you do not puncture any of these in the process. Pulling these out of the way will make it easier to cut through the diaphragm so that you can sever the esophagus. Now, remove the lungs and remaining innards by pulling everything downward. The inside of the carcass should be washed thoroughly afterward.

It is good to hang and drain the blood out of the meat at this time. Larger animals should be suspended upside down with the hind legs spread apart. Catch the blood in a container so that it can be boiled to replenish salts, vitamins, and other minerals. Hanging the animal for a time will also rid the body of parasites and make it easier to keep the meat clean while skinning.

The useful organs can be processed and cooked while the blood is draining. If the liver is not spotted or discolored, remove the bile bladder from the center. Lightly cook the meat right away for eating. It is packed with vitamins, minerals, and some fats.

Clean the kidneys and cut them in half before cooking. Soaking them for a time in cool water will improve the flavor. Boil them with the surrounding fat. They are high in protein, B vitamins, and minerals.

The heart should be cut to drain the blood and then boiled or roasted. It has a higher concentration of protein, vitamins, and minerals than other muscle tissue.

After the body has bled out and hung for a while, you will need to remove the hide. A lot of small game can have the skin pulled free of the body quite easily. With animals of greater size, you will need to cut the hide off by working outward from the incisions that you made to gut it. Cut it away from the body so that you can make your way around the legs and neck.

The animal's head can be a valuable source of nourishment as well. It may come across as distasteful, but the tongue, cheeks, eyes, and brain have been consumed for centuries and in many countries are still regarded as the prized portions of the animal.

The tongue can be softened by giving it a long boil. After it has cooled, the rough outer skin can be easily peeled off before eating. The meat and broth will have a very high-fat content with vitamins and minerals as well.

Larger animals can have plenty of meat in the cheek and jaw area that you will not want to waste. If there is not a large enough container to cook the entire head, cut as much of the fat and meat away so that it can be simmered with the tongue. The greatest value of this meat is the important fat which is normally found in lower quantities throughout the rest of a wild game animal's body.

The eyes can be boiled as well but do not eat the plastic-like disk of the retina. For most this can be the hardest portion to accept as food. The fluids inside are good but if you have plenty of water it is fine to use them for bait instead.

The brains can be equally unsettling but the only reason that you should pass on this one is if you intend to use it for tanning the animals hide. It is said that the brain of every animal can be used to sufficiently tan its own hide, but this is an extensive process that involves a good deal of skill and time. Boil or fry the brain to take advantage of the copious amounts of vitamins, minerals, and fat.

For the body, you may need to divide it for more convenient and faster cooking. Cutting around the muscle where the joints connect the legs to the body will allow you to separate portions. Small animals can be roasted whole or portioned for boiling.

Any larger bones should always be split to get at the marrow inside. The marrow is a superb fat replacement and provides nutrients that promote healthy body function on a huge scale. Remember that if the bones are split carefully, they can be used to make countless different functional tools. With some shaping, grinding, and carving you can construct valuable lures, hooks, spear points, utensils, and cutting items to name a few.

PRESERVATION

Many of the foods that you come across can be made to last for later meals. Most plant parts can be dried in the sun and wind. Thinly slicing various fruits, berries, tubers, and roots will let you dry them faster. When there is a lack of direct sunlight, use a stone that is heated near the low-burning coals of your fire to force the moisture out. The end result should be dry and firm.

I had a dried plum puree from Bulgaria that lasted close to a year without a problem. Well dried fruit should last over six months and most plants will keep even longer. Dry leaves and plant stalks are light to carry and normally do not attract the attention of scavenging animals. These are great to add into soups or broth. Fruits, nuts, and seeds will need you to take more care with them because rodents will sniff them out and chew through your gear to get at the food.

Slow roasting insects above the fire can make them last longer as well. Things like worms will dry better in the sun or on a heated stone. Dry insects are easy to crush and powder so that they can be thrown into a soup. Some hearty insects such as beetles and grasshoppers can be put into a container with breathing holes and a bit of vegetation to store live for a few days. Live storage can work for certain small animals that you catch in buried bottle traps as well. A day or two is about the limit with this method. In cooler temperatures, hard-boiled eggs should also last for a day or two when left inside the shell.

Sometimes you may have some extra meat scraps, catch a large animal, or have an environmental situation that directs you to save some of that meat. Preserving meat takes a bit more attention. The meat needs to be lean or have the fat cut away. Cut very thin strips that follow the grain of the meat for best results. It is good to rub the meat with salt or a bit of blood to act as a natural preservative.

Meat can be air dried in the sunlight, but this takes a long time and you need to keep the bugs away from it. It is better to force dry the meat over indirect heat by hanging it over the coals or using a hot stone. The meat will need to be turned regularly to ensure that it dehydrates evenly. When it is crisp, this method should give you a result that will last you about four or five days if it is kept away from moisture.

The best way to preserve meat is by smoking it. The smoke will coat the meat with an additional protective layer. This process is more complicated and doesn't always go quite right without practice. It also means that you will need to build a framework and rack that will hold your meat over the fire. That will, in turn, require canvas or other material to enclose your rack so that the meat is enveloped with smoke on the inside.

If all these materials are available, you will need to burn down a strong fire into a healthy bed of coals. Cover the coals with a previously gathered pile of green leaves that are not poisonous. Your rack will go above the pile of leaf-covered coals and then enclosed with the canvas. This will need to be constantly monitored to make sure that the coals continue to smolder but do not flare up and burn down the whole operation. You may need to add more leaves if the coals are too hot or build a second fire so that you can relocate the rack if the original coals burn down and stop smoking.

Two days of heavy smoking can give you meat that will last from two to four weeks if everything works properly. This process is a large expenditure and I would almost always recommend that you use the much easier method of forced dehydration.

Fish can be dried but it is usually best to eat them fresh. Any mollusks and crustaceans will need to be prepared and eaten immediately because they spoil rapidly. Other foods that you are not sure about preserving are better off eaten right away and not potentially wasted.

There are times when food preservation can be very important, but it can also pose an unwanted risk from scavengers. Being constantly watchful should keep you well-fed. Take only what you need. Remember that a regular supply of small morsels will adequately keep your internal fire burning the way that it was naturally intended.

DIRT TIME

Knowledge about survival food is a multifaceted piece of the puzzle. You can go a long way with the information that is outlined here but proficiency will require deliberate learning. Seek out the specific details that pertain to your region and make notes to go with your guide. Get acquainted with the plants, animals, and insects of your area. Know which are poisonous, edible, and dangerous. Understand their habits and individual needs. Think about the signs and indicators that can lead you to them.

The story about foraging, at the beginning of this chapter, has some important lessons. Even at our skill level, we had some doubt when we went out to the woods. This is all right, but only if you choose to overcome it. We reinforced our learning with a proven source of knowledge. Take the plant guide when you go out but if you do not also have the tracking and trapping skill, you will want books about those topics as well. These books will give you many pictures and indicators that you need to be aware of.

The dirt time itself brought us a lot of value. Naturally, we increased our skill level and knowledge kit but most importantly, it gave us the confidence in our ability to succeed. All these things can benefit the highly proficient and those with no training at all. The main thing is making a choice to take action against your limitations.

Going out and combining this knowledge into practiced learning is better done with companions. Bring friends or family and turn your observing into a challenging game. Take your time with the process and think through your actions. How you find different sources of food is just as important as the food itself. When doing these things for practice, try not to disrupt the environment too much with your activities. Take only what you need and replace things that you disturbed. Use what you learn to gain a greater understanding of the ecosystem, and it will be easier to become a part of it when you need to.

HUNTING

"THERE'S AN ABSOLUTE SURETY TO THE HANDS-ON CONSERVATION LIFESTYLE OF HUNTING, FISHING, AND TRAPPING WHERE YOU KNOW YOU'RE GOING TO CONSUME TODAY."

—TED NUGENT

Simply defined, hunting is an act of utilizing knowledge, gathered inputs, and certain tools to track down and capture prey. Many of the informational tidbits in the food chapter, especially the practice from the dirt time, will play an instrumental role here. This is where a deep understanding of the animal and its environment culminates into something greater.

Hunting is something that was born out of necessity. It comes from a time when we were just as much a part of the ecosystem as the animals that we hunted. A mutual respect was understood because those animals played an integral part in our survival. It was clear that we were all portions of the same great picture.

To a large degree, the grocery store and modern convenience have stolen away our appreciation for the ways that the world provides for us. This lack of understanding has led to complacency and indifference, for which the ecosystem has become massively degraded on a global scale. It has created an ever-widening rift between the feelings and empathy for the world which we are part of. As the distance between our relationship with nature expands, the situation becomes dire.

It is my hope that some things that you are learning here can put more of us onto a path where an intimacy with nature is held in higher esteem.

TRAIL SIGNS

Indicators abound for the conscientious observer. Sometimes they are glaringly obvious, and others will be cloaked with minuscule obscurity. With continued effort, more of these signs will begin to reveal themselves to you.

Initially, you will look for heavily trodden paths. These will often lead you to the places where animals eat, drink, and shelter. They can give an indication of the size of the animals that use these paths and their numbers. Watching the drinking places and feeding grounds will help you learn the times when the animals are most active. Often, you will find that only birds and large game are active during the daylight hours. Most small animals come out during dusk, nighttime, and early morning.

Knowing the feeding grounds will give you better chances to encounter your prey. If you have a grasp of what they are eating and can locate that food source, you will also find the animals. Not only that, their food source might be something that you can eat as well. They may lead you to food indirectly. Some animals can eat things which will poison you so make sure to know it or test it.

Some signs of feeding can include nut shells, chewed bark, seed husks, fruit peels, upturned ground, nibbled fungus and broken plants. It could also be something like the carapace of a crustacean that was left by a raccoon or the bones of a small rodent that was discarded by a scavenging bird.

Animal droppings can share a wealth of knowledge about the animals and what they are eating. Fresh droppings will have moisture and a smell. This will tell you that it was more recent, and the animal may still be close. If it is dry and odorless, the scat is old. Break it apart to see what is inside. Are there seeds and plant material? Is it mostly woody or do you see fur and small bones? A bluish or purple color can tell you that it was eating berries. The size of the waste can also give you a general indication of the animal's size.

Locating the places where they drink will give you another focus point. Just like you, the animals need that water and they will come back to it. A lot of animals will drink in the morning or in the evening after feeding. If it is a spot that they frequent, the animal can view it as a place of relative safety which can give you a slight advantage. Occasionally, the trails that lead to water will also be used as crossings. You might be shown an easier path through difficult terrain by those who know the land better than you.

When you find a trail leading to an active burrow or den, you have also found a location where that animal will assuredly be coming and going. Perhaps it is a burrow where fresh dirt has been excavated. You may see a hole in a tree where the shells from food have been thrown below. Less obvious are the small trails that lead under a rock or pile of stones. Maybe it is a narrow tunnel leading into thick vegetation or dense brambles. Regardless of location, finding the place where an animal shelters will pinpoint concentrated activity.

In time, you will begin to notice more trails around you. The places where the bark has been scraped off trees by passing squirrels will stand out. A bruised leaf on a plant that got stepped on will catch your eye. The absence of dew on the moss where a mouse ran across the log will be like a highlighted line on a white page. The less obvious trails left by individual animals in a single passing are the hardest to spot but the signs are there if you know how to look for them.

TRACKING

The art of tracking can be developed to such a great degree that it will seem magical when viewed by the casual observer. If you want to be blown away by the depth of tracking mastery, look up a man named Tom Brown Jr. He is a master in the field of survival and especially tracking. His various books and field guides are highly recommended for greater learning and The Tracker Wilderness Survival School that he runs is exemplary.

Everything leaves a trace of its passing without fail. Even the minute steps of an ant left in the dust on a windowpane can be followed. Age, size, weight, speed, health, disposition, and species just scratch the surface of the information that can be found within the story of a single track. Tracking is an ancient science that is a timeless aspect of hunting ability.

In truth, learning trail signs is a soft introduction to the tracking process. Unraveling some of the greater mysteries about tracking can take a lifetime of intense dedication. I do not expect that of you. Surely, though, you can look more closely at these tracks to identify what kind of animal you are dealing with.

Every species has an identifying signature in the shape of their track. All of them are unique in some way. There are groupings with similarities like hooves or paws. Others may be webbed or closely resemble hands. Just like our hands and feet, many animals have noticeable discrepancies between their front and hind feet.

Coupled with the individual track, you can also take things from the pattern in a grouping of tracks to help you identify things about your prey. Animals move in various ways that leave a pattern which will often specify them. Distance between them, depth of the track, and the way their feet came into contact with the ground can tell you if it was walking, running, or stalking. Understanding the movement groupings of tracks can be very helpful.

Knowing the animal droppings is another important thing to grasp. Not only does this lead you to the food source, but each species will have a unique size and shape to their droppings that can help you pinpoint which animal it is. Scat can be used to tell you if the animal is adequately hydrated, in good health, and if it is an adult or youth.

Tracks that are left in wet sand, soft mud, and snow will leave the best imprints and pattern groupings. As a beginner, walking along shorelines and the banks of any body of water will give you the fastest learning. Going out the day after a light snow has fallen is superb for tracking. It is exciting when you are able to unravel the mystery of exactly what happened on the trail that you follow.

At times, it will completely baffle you and other times you will be totally amazed by the story that opens before you. I still remember how cool it was the first time that I found a spot where the journey of a mouse through the snow was suddenly interrupted by the swooping talons of a hungry owl. Better yet, was the time that I was out with my daughter. We followed a pattern of subtle lines swiped into the snow. She was able to figure out that they were left by the wingtips of a low-flying bird. The tracks brought us to the place where the spring melt had partially opened a small stream and the crow had landed to get a drink.

Tracking skill is a valuable tool that will assist you immensely even when it is honed to a small degree. With practice, you find that time has left tracks everywhere. Smooth stones polished by the beating of waves, the bend in a tree which was battered by constant wind, rust corroded metal, a valley dug by a winding river, and the scars on your hand, these are all things that reveal something to those who take the time to notice. Follow the tracks.

WEAPONS

You can enhance your success in hunting by using certain weapons. There is also the chance you will need these weapons for protection. Our ancestors were well aware of the risk involved with animal encounters and as a result, quickly adopted the use of rudimentary weapons. Rocks, clubs, spears, and throwing sticks were the first to be developed. As time progressed, improvements were made, and these tools became more complex and extremely functional. It has brought us to an age where high-quality knives, crossbows, and firearms are the standard.

MODERN WEAPONS

If by chance you have a firearm, bow, or crossbow with you, use ammunition intelligently. Neither squander ammunition nor use it to take game that is larger than necessity dictates. In certain environments, these tools might be more important for protection. Only use them when there is a serious need for food or plentiful ammunition. Remember that the sound of a gunshot is a good way to alert distant rescuers of your location.

ROCK

Despite its brutal simplicity, a well-thrown rock is still stunningly effective. Something that is rounded and fits nicely into your hand will work the best. The force that is dispersed upon impact is great enough to stagger or kill most small to medium-sized animals. A dazed or wounded animal is easier to catch and finish off. Rocks will also work to deter large predators. It is always a good idea to keep a few placed by your shelter area. Nothing likes to get hit by a rock.

THROWING STICK

The principle behind a throwing stick is like that of a rock. For hunting, this weapon will be more suitable. It is lighter to carry a few of these which saves energy. They have increased surface area which will improve your chances to hit the target. These sticks are also easy to retrieve after throwing, so you can use them many times.

Use heavy wood that is durable when making throwing sticks. Place your forefinger and thumb together in a circle to get the correct diameter. The length should be equal to the distance between the crook of your elbow to the fingertips. Shave off the bark and whittle down any protrusions so that it will move through the air cleanly.

These will be predominantly used for taking down small game but can work with larger animals as well. Most of the time you will want to throw with a sidearm to take advantage of the surface area. Stand with your throwing arm behind you and try not to wind up or flag your motion during the throw because it will startle your prey. Carry three or four throwing sticks in case you need to take more than one shot.

BOLAS

Another fine throwing weapon, the bolas is used to entangle and subdue game at a medium range. This can be very effective against larger birds and waterfowl. It can even trip and bring down large game if thrown at the legs. You will have the best luck using this against groups of animals.

To make a bola, you will need three arm length strands of strong cordage that can be tied without breaking. Parachute cord is perfect. Find three oblong stones that you can almost close your hand around. It is best if the stone has a bit of a ridge so that your knot does not slip off. If you can chip or grind away a groove in the canter, that works nicely. You will want solid stones that are dense and do not break easily.

A lashing must be secured very tightly to each of the stones. Three knotted wraps will create more surface friction and will be less likely to slip or loosen. The three long ends of your cordage will then be tied together with a snug overhand knot. When thrown, the stones will separate in the air and then wrap around the target when they make contact with it.

Use care when implementing this weapon because a mistake could result in serious head injury. Its use is intended for open areas that are free of branches and tall brush which can disrupt the trajectory. To throw the bolas, hold the knotted end well overhead and swing it in a circular motion by turning your wrist instead of the whole arm. The spinning motion must go back over your head and come forward away from your body. To spin it the other way will complicate the throw and your aim.

When you are ready to throw, the spin will bring the stones forward and you will lead in with your arm for the release. Be ready to chase in behind it to finish the kill before it can untangle itself and escape. Before adapting to this irregular throwing technique, expect some struggle. My first attempts at using this weapon yielded some wild throws that were not even close to the target and almost resulted in a broken window. It can be a bit tricky, so practice this away from people or things that shouldn't be damaged.

CLUB

A decent club or cudgel is easy to make or improvise from materials on hand. A sturdy chunk of branch that resembles a baseball bat is perfect. Don't rule out a salvaged board, metal pipe, or the lug wrench from your car. Just make sure that whatever you choose is strong enough to withstand a heavy impact without breaking. It should also be light enough that you do not struggle when you handle it.

A club can be used to take down animals that you can get close to. There are times that you can use it to get fish in shallow water. The short range of this weapon dictates that you will mostly use it on slow-moving animals and to finish the things that you have stunned or disabled by other means. Injured animals will aggressively protect themselves, so the club can give you a safe distance to complete the kill. Remember that these weapons are devastatingly powerful, so make sure that you do not mutilate your dinner.

BRANCH SWATTER

For small animals that are fast and hard to catch, you can make a branch to swat at them. Pine boughs that have close branches which spread out flat work effectively. Certain palm fronds are good as well. Trim the branch down to something which can be maneuvered easily. The idea is to stun the animal and hold it in place. Use these to capture small game like frogs, lizards, crabs, snakes, and sometimes little rodents. If you use this to hold a snake down, make sure that you also club it in the head and pin it in place before getting close.

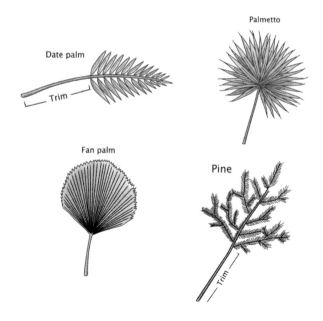

SPEAR

The spear is another age-old weapon that can be simple or specialized, but either way, it is an implicitly versatile item. A basic spear will be slightly taller than you are and have a sharpened point at one end. Select a sturdy hardwood sapling to work with. The straight shaft should be about the diameter of your index finger to the bend of the joint in your thumb. Shave away any rough portions or protrusions on the shaft. Carve one end into a twenty-five to thirty-degree point and the other into a rounded stub.

Fit into notch

Metal rod

The ends should be fire-hardened to give them added strength. Spend at least an hour turning each end over the heat from burning coals. You do not want to blacken or burn the wood, but it will take on a light tan or brown coloration as the wood slowly dries.

Take the time to construct a quality spear and it will serve you well. For close range, the point will be used for piercing thrusts and the butt-end to strike or club with. A spear is also good for pinning down a snake or wounded animal. When defending yourself, it has a long range that can deliver fast and powerful strikes.

Carved bone

Practice throwing at something that will not destroy the point like a soft rotten log, and it will become useful at medium range. Turned sideways, you will hold the spear slightly closer to the butt-end with your backhand so that it balances properly. With the shaft along the side of your head thrust forward and release as your body turns to face the target. Start with the target close and increase the throwing strength and distance as your accuracy improves. Keep the point sharpened and it will be good enough to penetrate animal hide just the way it is.

After my knife, the spear is my first weapon choice because it can serve many other needs. While traveling, it is great for balance or to probe areas that could be unsafe to step. A spear will provide stability during water crossings or if you need something extra to push off of when going over obstacles. In a pinch, it will become the ridge for a shelter or a signal to wave with a bright piece of cloth attached to it. As situations unfold you will be surprised by many of the other uses.

Flat metal

There are numerous things that you can use to modify and specialize in different spear tips. Flat metal, bone shards, sharp stone, and a metal rod are a few things that can be used. Never use your knife because it is far too valuable as a cutting tool and can be lost or damaged when attached to a spear. I will recommend that you stick to using the basic spear described above.

Stone/glass

Properly securing different spear tips can be difficult and time-consuming. In addition to that, they generally do not hold up to long-term abuse. Something that can be easily remade or simply carved to a new point is more practical. The pictures of the improvised spear points have been provided because there may be times that it could suit your needs.

KNIFE

At a very close range, the knife that you carry is a weapon that should be used wisely. It is the perfect thing to use when you need to quickly end the suffering of any animals that you knocked unconscious, wounded, or pinned down. Severing the vital artery beneath the throat, driving your blade into the brain stem, or simply removing the entire head can be the most efficient way to complete the task. Make absolutely sure that the animal is no longer a danger to you before bringing your hand into close proximity.

When using a knife for protection from an animal assailant, you will need to move with rapid precision. Most animals will not attack unless they are rabid, large predators, protecting their young or cornered and scared. If they come after you, make no mistake, they mean business. If it is at your side where it belongs, that knife might just be your last resort. Try to puncture the lungs or stab into vital arteries. It is best to repeatedly stab and cut outward. Trying to slash and cut will be largely ineffective against animals with fur and tough hide.

Keep in mind that your knife is the most important physical tool that you have, so do not do anything that could risk damaging or losing it while hunting. It is best when used to complement the hunting by building your weapons and preparing your game for cooking.

OTHER TOOLS

There are several things that can be used to assist your hunting at certain times. When night hunting, a torch or flashlight will sometimes draw in or temporarily mesmerize certain animals. Game can be chased along a trail where you placed netting, brush, or tangles of vine that can slow them down enough for a kill. At times, you can use smoke to drive animals out of their burrows and hiding spots. There are also places where you can utilize the terrain and direct game into falling over blind crevices or into holes where they become injured.

Take advantage of natural conditions when you are able. Moving when the sun is low and at your back can obscure your position and keep the prey from spotting you. The noise from strong wind or moving water will cover movement and keep you from being heard. Try to stay downwind so that your sound and smell are not carried in the animal's direction. Use things from the surroundings to conceal your movement when stalking or make camouflaging and blinds to hide behind.

FISHING

First, it is important to understand some basic habits of fish. In warmer temperatures, they will often seek out cooler water. This leads them to deeper water, the outside bends of rivers, shaded overhanging banks, the shelter of aquatic plants and beneath trees that have fallen into the water. In the morning and evening, they are often in shallow water feeding and this is the best time to try your luck. When it is cold, the fish will move to warmer water near the surface or even into sunny places.

Where water is flowing, fish will face upstream so that the water moves naturally through their gills and to better see food that is coming their way. They also prefer places where there is more oxygen in the water. After rapids, below waterfalls and where rivers enter a lake are good places for fishing. When I was young, we would go to a wide place in the river that had a long stretch of shallow rapids. This ankle-deep water was the best place to spear fish as they struggled to escape amidst the many rocks.

These animals are almost always skittish and will retreat at the first sign of abnormality in their habitat. Don't cast a shadow into the water. Vibrations and noises when moving along the bank or through the water will cause them to flee. Refraction through the water gives them a superior line of visibility to the shore so you need to keep low, or they will spot you. Picture a heron or egret stalking through the water. After one gentle step, they watch patiently for a long time before taking another.

Fish are naturally curious because it often leads them to food. Subtle movement in the water can catch their eye. Shiny and reflective things can bring them to investigate. Pieces of aluminum, for instance, can be placed in the water at your fishing spot. When the sun causes reflective flashes of light it can draw the fish in. A torch or flashlight shined into the water at night can also attract fish to be netted, clubbed, or speared.

Signs of feeding will be helpful as well. Look for the places where they are jumping or nipping at things on the surface. Take note of the times when this is happening and try to observe what they are feeding upon. The diet of fish will often follow the hatching and life stages of smaller prey, whether it be insect, amphibian, or other fish. Knowing these foods will lead you to the fish. One of the best secrets to any type of hunting is to understand the needs of your prey and how they are interconnected with all the other pieces of the ecosystem.

The standard form of fishing is with a net or a pole, line, and hook. The correct branch can become a pole. Hooks and lures can be easily fashioned from many things. Almost every time, the hang-up is going to be obtaining a suitable line. Good nets can be tough to make but many things can be turned into a substantial net.

Poles are useful for numerous reasons. They can extend your reach into otherwise precarious places where the fish may hide. A pole can give additional leverage when bringing in sizable fish or help you set the hook after the fish has bitten. It can also be handy to use a pole when trying to mimic the motions of the fishes' food source with your bait. Probably the most important thing is the pole's ability to obscure your position from your watchful prey. Select a straight pole from strong and flexible green wood. A good pole length will measure from the ground to the tips of your fingers when your arm is raised overhead. The trunk of a young sapling works best.

Lures and hook possibilities are only limited by your imagination. With one aluminum can and a multi-tool, you can make a wide selection of lures to try. Things such as safety pins, paper clips, and pieces of wire are perfect for hooks. You can also make legitimate hooks from certain plant thorns or tiny animal bones.

One of the best is a simple gorge hook which can be made quickly in the desired size from a piece of stick. Tie a line in the center of a gorge hook and slide the bait over it. When the bait is taken, the hook will turn inside the fish and lodge there. Incorporating things like feathers, bits of cloth or something shiny to your lure can be helpful as well. Smaller hooks and lures will give you better chances to catch all sizes of fish.

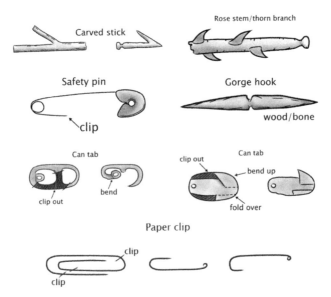

There are several kinds of smaller tie-down rope that you can unravel or separate into the fine strands it is made from. A good example is parachute or 550 cord. It has seven small strands that can each be separated into thin lines that work well for fishing. Because of its strength and versatility when broken down, I keep a generous amount stashed anywhere that it could prove useful.

Sometimes you might be able to salvage thin wire or weave plant fibers together. There could be a line on your equipment or even the string from your sweatshirt. The problems with making fishing line will be getting something thin enough to affix on a lure and not alert the fish yet strong enough to do the intended job. Then, it needs to be of a length that will function. More often you will have thicker strands of material that are short. These will generally be wisely implemented in the crafting of other tools. This does not mean that you should abandon pole and line fishing as a possibility, but there is likely a better way to catch fish than the one with which you are most familiar.

If you have the available materials, you could construct an intricate gill net that is able to span a fair distance in the water. It must be strong, and the holes need to be small enough to trap the fish. This takes skill, time and resources. Generally, it's not necessary. Implemented correctly, a simple dip net made from a forked branch with a shirt tied over it is more practical and something that can be used to catch many other kinds of small game. If it is made with salvaged fabric, you can poke some small holes to let the water pass through better. It can also be made with cordage if you do not have the fabric.

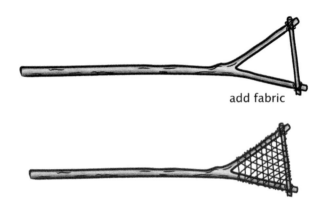

add fabric

Instead of using large nets, it is easier to herd fish into a strategic catch point. In shallow areas of most rivers and streams, it is possible to direct fish by driving wooden stakes across the water diagonally. Leave just enough space between them so that the fish will not want to go through. Reeds or long grasses can be woven between the stakes to close the gaps. This will drive them to the far end of the blockade where you can make a corral to trap them or force the fish into a shallow bank where you can use your pole net to scoop them up.

Once the catch point has been placed, it is just a matter of going upstream some ways and then walking downstream through the water to send them toward it. Splash branches in the water and cause a ruckus as you go to scare as many fish as possible. Those driven to the catch point can be speared, netted or even caught by hand. Clubbing is also effective or sometimes slapping a broad flat object on the surface of the water will cause a concussion that temporarily stuns the fish for easy collection.

The catch point can be reused after a day or coming from farther upstream can bring more fish. If the results are not good, pull the stakes and relocate it to a different position. This method can be one of the easiest ways to catch fish. It is not a complicated process and there are almost always branches that can be used for stakes. When there are no branches, you can also do this with rocks in the shallows but make sure that you have it in a good position because it will take more work and can't be relocated easily.

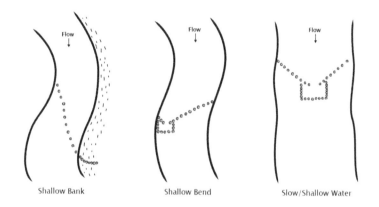

Shallow Bank   Shallow Bend   Slow/Shallow Water

A similar catch point can be used on the shore of the ocean. A tidal trap works best on areas of shoreline where the water is not very deep. A tightly placed row of stakes in a curved shape works well, but you can use rocks here, too. The placement should be just above the low-tide line. Long stakes that are driven in deeply will ensure that they stay in place. If there are strong waves, it can be problematic so try to choose a location that is calmer.

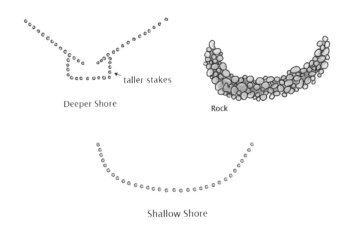

taller stakes

Deeper Shore

Rock

Shallow Shore

Make a bunch of these traps to increase your odds. When the high tide moves out fish and other sea life will be caught in your trap. Make sure that you are there as the tide recedes. The shoreline is regularly scavenged by many animals who will happily eat your lunch or certain things like a juicy crab might just walk away.

If you can find or salvage any plastic bottles, they are handy for catching small fish. Cut the top off the bottle and place a rock and some bait inside. The top will then be flipped over and slid into the bottle. Two pairs of angled cuts where the top fits into the bottle in opposite directions will make small tabs that allow you to lock the bottle top into place. A small water bottle can catch plentiful minnows. With larger bottles, you can also cut off the mouth of the bottle to catch something bigger. The rock inside will hold the bottle at the bottom but also pile some rocks on the sides and top to keep it in position. Places that are shallow and calm will easily give you a meal of many small morsels.

Spearing fish is an art unto itself. This only works with fish that have bodies which are the size of your hand and larger. Sometimes the conditions are perfect for this approach. Spawning or times when the water level is low can conveniently trap big fish in shallow water. Occasionally fish can be driven into trickling rapids, tidal flats, or gradual shorelines. These situations can be ideal.

Stalking the waters or spearing by torchlight can be downright harrowing. It takes serious patience and very slow movements. Be mindful of your shadow. Be close enough to make an explosive thrust that will be able to push all the way to the bottom. Before you strike, get the tip of the spear into the surface of the water. This will help to prevent the water from diverting your shot. Remember to aim just below the fish to account for the visual displacement of refraction. When you strike, drive the spear to the bottom and pin the fish in place. Reach under the fish and hold it securely before lifting the spear and fish out of the water together. This will take diligence, but if the fish are there just keep trying.

Another trick that works when fish are in a confined area, but hard to get at, is to muddy the water. Kicking up mud and silt from the bottom or mixing in copious amounts of soil from the shore will degrade the water quality. This is displeasing to the fish and makes it hard to process oxygen through their gills. As a result, they will come to the surface. At this time, you can use a spear, gently scoop them up with a pole net, or slowly bring your hands underneath the fish and throw it onto the bank.

There are times when baiting fish into places where they can be easily caught is an effective practice. Regularly placing insects, pieces of animal innards or food scraps into a certain area might bring the fish to that place. When it is warm enough for flies, you can entangle animal innards onto a branch and stake it above the water. After a few days, the larvae of the flies will begin to fall into the water and the fish will come to feed. Be sure to use good judgment and do this well away from your camp, as it can also bring in predators that you do not want in your area.

In the winter, fish like to stay near shallow water, so it is possible to icefish a short distance from the shore when the ice is strong enough to support your weight. Always use caution when on the ice. Take a long and sturdy wooden staff to help you get out if the ice breaks and if you are able, secure a rope to a tree or something anchored on the shore. Build a fire to help you melt a hole through the ice with heated rocks. Make sure that the fire is kept burning while you are fishing just in case you break through. Ice fishing works best with a hook and line, but it is possible to attract fish with a torch at night for spearing.

A standard spear can work for fishing, but you will be better off with a spear that is more slender and has multiple barbed points that spread outward at the end. Connect your index finger to the joint where your thumb comes off your hand for the right diameter and look for a straight green shaft that is about your height. Tie a strong wrap of cordage around one end of the shaft about one hand length down. Push the blade of your knife into the butt to start a split in the center of the shaft. Make another cut crossways that will divide the shaft into quarters. Gently spread the divisions apart until the splits run down to your wrap of cordage.

Now, you will want to soak the end in warm water so that it becomes more pliable. While you are waiting, you can whittle down two short pieces of the stick that will be pushed down into the splits to force them apart. Start with pieces that are about the size of your little finger and adjust if needed. When the soaking is done, you will need to carefully force the dowels down between the split sections without breaking them off. Once the dowels are in place they will need to be tied and wrapped securely with cordage.

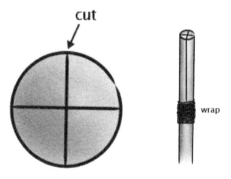

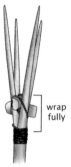

wrap
fully

At this time, you will sharpen the points. Carve barbs into them if you can do so without compromising the strength of the tip. Having barbs can be helpful in deeper water but in shallows, it is better to have strong points that will not break when pushed into the bottom to pin the fish. This spear is more delicate and driving it down too hard can break it, especially when it is rocky. A quick thrust will penetrate the fish and does not need to be extremely forceful. The separate points will give you much better chances to hit the fish.

TRAPS & SNARES

There is a strong potential to do better with traps and snares than with standard hunting methods. They give you the distinct opportunity to multiply your efforts by being in many places at once and working while you are not there. Knowing this, you will also have to understand that setting many of them will increase your probability of success. Rub all the working parts of these mechanisms with dirt or scat to mask your scent. When you place traps and snares it is important that you disturb the area as little as possible.

It is crucial to check these locations on a regular basis. You do not want the animal to struggle free or possibly be taken by another predator. If the prey is not killed by your device, it is also not prudent to allow them to suffer any longer than necessary. If you are hungry enough to use traps, you need to be responsible enough to check them.

When you set traps and snares, the places of focused activity will give you the best chances. Spots where the plant life narrows into a choke point on a busy game trail are optimal. A short distance from the burrow is also good, but do not set it too close because animals are more cautious when emerging. The paths that lead to and from the drinking places or feeding grounds are functional as well.

Try to have a system of organization when emplacing traps and snares. It is easy to forget where you set and camouflaged these items in a landscape that can have similar features. Construct a small map by making marks with your knife into a piece of bark to help you remember if need be. Also, make sure that everyone in the group knows where the traps are set, so they are not set off accidentally.

You will need to use the best judgment about which application will practically suit the environment that you are dealing with. Expect technical adjustments and progressive trial until you achieve familiarity.

Remember that there are very few places where setting these types of traps and snares is legal outside the exception of a true emergency. They should never be implemented unless there is a true need. It is all right to practice setting them up at home if you take them down when you are done. If you are caught practicing in the wild, there could be serious legal implications.

PIT TRAP

This simple trap requires little more than the time to dig a hole. The size will depend on what you are trying to catch. This is best used for lower food chain creatures and small game. Larger animals have more capability of escaping, and you will need to do some serious digging which burns a lot of time and energy.

Place the freshly dug ground onto your poncho and use it for your shelter or fire ring. The sides of your pit should be somewhat inverted so that the top is narrower than the bottom. This will serve as prevention from things climbing out. Placing bait at the bottom of the hole will draw interest to the area.

Place dry leaves, grass or some lose ground around the mouth of the hole so that it slips away when the animal begins to fall. A few blades of grass can cover the hole, but it does not need to be completely hidden. Many animals will just go into the hole for food with the belief that they can get back out. A rock or log that is propped over the hole will encourage small animals to go underneath for shelter and keep them from jumping out after they have fallen into the hole.

BOTTLE PIT

It is disappointing that plastic bottles can be found littering many wilderness areas and washed up on coastlines. The good news is that these bottles can be salvaged into a multitude of useful survival tools. An excellent thing to do with these is to make another version of the pit trap. Bottle traps can have an advantage because the slippery sides are very hard for creatures to climb out of. They are also very effective in places where the ground is too loose to hold the sides of a pit or it is saturated, and the pit fills with water after being dug.

Cut the top from the bottle to widen the opening but do not discard it because you can use the same bottle to catch small fish. Dig a hole and bury the bottle to make your pit trap. Add some bait and prepare the outer rim in the same fashion as you would an ordinary pit trap. Larger bottles and jugs will give you the opportunity to get bigger animals.

Bait

Remember to take the bottle if you move on. It can be reused for trapping, collecting water, or a storage container.

Rock/log

Bottle

Bait

Pit traps work for catching insects, reptiles, and small rodents. A baited bottle trap can be a great way to catch scavenging crabs on the coastline. Be cautious when you check these traps because the animals that you catch will still be alive and it might just be a scorpion or poisonous snake. If it is something dangerous, you may just need to cover the hole and fill it with water to drown your prey.

DEADFALL TRAP

The idea of this trap is to get the animal to disengage a mechanism that will cause a weighted object to fall onto them and either kill or trap the animal in place. The basic concept involves a tripwire or baited release mechanism. Crushing force will often come from a heavy log or rock that is propped up or suspended. Once you grasp the function of this trap you, will find that there are many creative variations that can be used.

The simplest way that I have found is to use two sticks and some bait in conjunction with your weighted object. Sharpen one stick to a point and carve a small notch into one end of the other stick where the point of the first will rest. Pin the bait against the underside of the weighted object with the notched stick and precariously stabilize the configuration in a propped fashion by fitting the point of the other stick into the notch.

When the animal tries to pull the bait free, the first stick should roll and release the prop to bring the weight crashing down upon it. Sometimes it may help to tie the bait to the stick, forcing the animal to pull harder. It may also help to put the bait at a height which will cause your prey to reach up on its hind legs. This will make it harder for the animal to dash away before impact. If you do not have bait, this same design can be used with a tripwire. The deadfall is then set at the choke point of a game trail or near the entrance to a burrow.

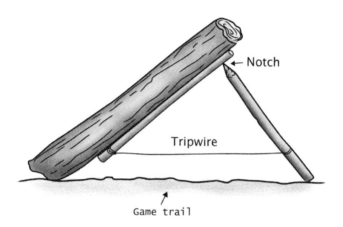

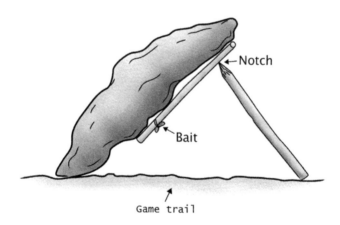

By poking branches into the ground, you can make funneled choke points in places where there are none. When using a deadfall, make sure that nothing besides the animal will obstruct the fall of your weighted object from making solid contact with the ground. With areas that have soft ground, it can also help to put some smaller rocks on the ground where the impact will take place. This can help to crush bones and make it harder for the animal to dig free.

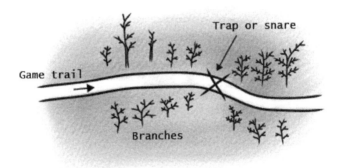

SNARES

What you want to achieve with the use of a snare is strangulation or catching part of the animal in a noose that will not allow it to get free. To build snares, you will need fine cordage that is very strong. A flexible wire is perfect, but the inner strands of parachute cord work as well. Certain plant fibers or animal gut can be used, but they must be resistant to breaking.

I will gauge the description of these snares to catching rabbits because they are found almost everywhere and are good targets for snares. Understand that any snare can be adjusted to the game that you seek to capture. Think about the size of the head and how far it is held above the ground when the animal moves.

The simplest of snares will just be a noose or slipknot tied into a loop that is about fist-sized or slightly larger than the animal's head. The other end will then be tied firmly in place around a small tree or a stake that cannot be jostled loose or yanked out. Suspend the open hole of the noose at head-height or about a hand-width above the game trail. Use dry twigs to hold the noose in place. These brittle twigs should break away if they become entangled with the noose and the animal. Green sticks can also be looked at as something the animal may want to chew on and consequently ruin the snare.

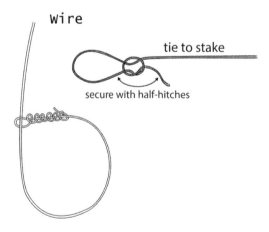

When tying the noose with cordage, you will make a simple overhand knot or half-hitch around the free running end of your line to create a loop that slips. It should leave just enough room for it to slide easily. Tie two more half-hitches over the working end to secure the first knot in place. With wire, make a small loop for the free running end to pass through. Continue with several circles around the back side of the loop and finish with a half-hitch that has the end bent over to lock it in place. There are quite a few ways to make the noose, but these should be easy for a beginner.

With the trap in place, the noose should begin to tighten when the animal's head passes through the loop. The natural reaction at this point will be to bolt or push forward which will secure the noose more tightly in place. If there is any brush close by, there is also a chance that it will become entangled and give it less opportunity to wriggle free.

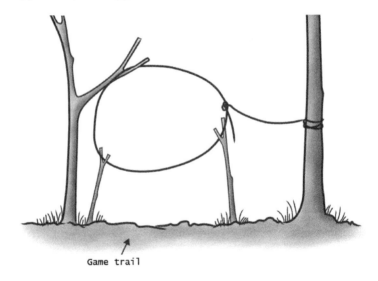

Game trail

SPRING SNARE

This device uses the same concept as the noose. Now the line is secured to a trigger that holds a pulled-down branch or bent over sapling which is also attached to the trigger. When the noose is pulled taut by the animal trying to escape, it will release the trigger. After the trigger is disengaged, it will release the tension on the branch and yank the prey off the ground. Pulling it from the ground tightens the noose and makes it very difficult to escape. Ideally, the sharp motion should snap the animal's neck and end its suffering. Suspending the animal will serve to keep the catch from being taken by another predator.

The trigger is made up of two parts. You will need a long stake with a forty-five-degree notch cut into the top end. The second part is the trigger peg. It will be about four fingers in length and have the lower end cut at a forty-five-degree angle. Above the angled cut you will carve a square notch that will allow it to fit over the top of the notch in the stake. It is also good to carve indentions that circle the trigger peg where the cordage will be tied. This will prevent the lines from slipping off.

This trigger design is intended to hold tension from directly above and release when pulled from the side. Slight adjustments can be made by angling the stake. Make sure that the stake is driven deeply enough to hold the tension. Turning it like a screw as you pound it in will make it hold more securely. If you lay the noose on the ground this snare can also be set up with a tripwire or a line that has bait tied to it.

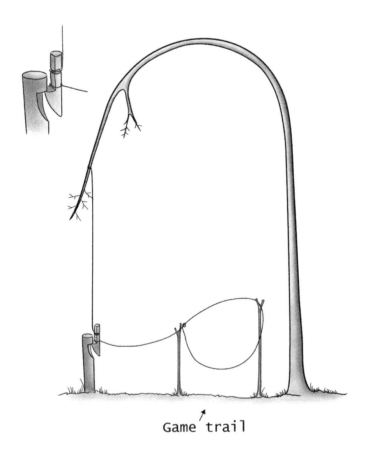

Game trail

DIRT TIME

In many ways, your hunting skills can be refined on a regular basis. Watch the animals and observe the things that they do. Notice the places they prefer, the way they move, and things they eat. Even the animals that live in urban environments follow certain routines concerning food and water. Look for the indicators that will show the trails that are frequently used. Don't forget to notice the birds, for they will reveal a great many things if you are sharp enough to take note.

Tracks are everywhere. Whether left by creature, wind, water, or time, you must notice them all. This one task will give you a heightened awareness that can be integrated into far more things than you can imagine. The process of taking in information from your surroundings and analyzing cause and effect will put you in touch with the roots of any environment. It is enlightening when you can slow down and figure out what happened by using the marks that were left behind.

When you are in the wilderness, focus your tracking skills on the creatures that would be potential food sources. Learn from the tracks of the rabbit and holes left in the tree by a woodpecker. One is a direct connection to food and the beetle larvae in the rotten tree is indirect, but the tracks led you there all the same. Get better at matching the track to the individual animal that left it. Practice in different seasons and look for more obscure tracks or details that will tell you more about the creatures that left them.

If you are anything like me, making primitive weapons and traps will be a fun project, especially when it is time to test them out. Consider how well they work, their durability, and your overall skill at using these things. Look at ways to improve the things that did not work and try to utilize various improvised materials.

Make targets for your weapons out of snow, rotten logs, or fruits and vegetables. Test your fishing spear by tying a cucumber to a rock and submerging it in the water. Try to rig a deadfall that substitutes the weight for a lightweight basket or cage that can trap something without harming it. The kids might have fun trying to catch the family cat under a laundry basket. Remember the "without harming it" part. Your significant other would not soon forgive you if poor Fluffy got knocked out! All joking aside, unnecessary stress and duress is also harmful. Some pets would care very little about getting trapped for a moment while others would easily scare and go into a panic. Use good judgment.

Practice with traps and snares in ways that you are legally allowed. Look for the places where you would be able to emplace them when you are out in the wilderness. Find the things that you can use to make them and bring the pieces home to work on. Set them up at home and see how well you can get them to work. Once you become skilled with the simple traps and snares described here, move on to trying your hand at some of the more complicated variations. Being adept with many kinds will give you more control when dealing with different circumstances.

NOTE: Before conducting hunting or trapping of any kind make sure that you check the regulations and abide by them. These laws have been emplaced for a reason and breaking them can result in severe penalties.

NAVIGATION

"BEING BRAVE ISN'T THE ABSENCE OF FEAR. BEING
BRAVE IS HAVING THAT FEAR BUT FINDING A WAY
THROUGH IT."

—BEAR GRYLLS

Not knowing where you are can be an overwhelming and fearful ordeal. Being lost in the wilderness when you are under-prepared and out of your element can be downright crippling. You need to find a way through the fear and your surroundings alike. This leads us all the way back to the beginning. Don't lose your head. Navigation is a game of calm and consistent thinking. There are always known variables that you can bring into play. Make a mental note of every known factor and begin to put together a usable framework.

There are few times when we have no general sense of our current location or where we came from. If you are arguing this, it may be time to reevaluate your extracurricular activities. At very least, you should be able to say which state or country you are in. Seriously though, there is a great likelihood that you will know approximately where you are most of the time.

Think about the major land features that are relative to your localized position. Are there major lakes or rivers that you know of? What cities or towns are in the general proximity? Are there identifiable things such as mountains, coastlines, or man-made structures that can give you guidance?

As you begin to compile information, it will need to be processed in conjunction with a map if you are fortunate enough to have one. If you do not have a map, then you need to start making a rough map. Use whatever is available. Obviously, paper and pencil are best, but it could be scratched into bark or done with coal on some fabric. When there is nothing to use, you will need to make a map on the ground. You may not be able to take it with you, but it will still help to get your bearings.

Once there is a general sense of position, it is good to evaluate the choice of movement or holding that position. Staying where you are might be the first place that people will look for you. Maybe there is immediate danger that will force you to move quickly. It is important to be supremely observant when rapidly moving through unfamiliar terrain.

The choice may be dependent upon the area's ability to sustain your needs. Sometimes you will have to hold movement because of weather, darkness or insufficient data about directional knowledge. You could just have to wait for darkness to give you a good look at the city lights reflecting off the clouds or a glimpse at the North Star.

DIRECTION

Having an idea of the cardinal directions is almost always a must when movement is necessary. The exception is when an imminent threat forces you to clear the area. Wandering blindly or walking in circles is always a bad thing. Obtaining directional reasoning will work together with your framework of known information. It should lead you to a few simple conclusions. If I head East, it will put me on the roadway. Moving North will bring me to the edge of the sea. There is an impassable marshland to the South-West and I can't go that way.

Many times, people will say that someone has a great natural sense of direction. This is something that works on two levels but rarely is it natural. In almost every case, it boils down to paying attention to certain inputs. The first level is largely memorization and familiarity. Just as you learn the streets of your town and surrounding area, someone who lives in an expanse of forest will come to know the features that give him a sense of location.

On a larger scale, you can talk to a semi-truck driver who makes deliveries throughout the United States. She could draw a map of the major roadways, the states that they run through, or where they connect and the cities that they lead to. This is a sense of direction. However, if you placed a truck driver into the woods, she would be just as confused as the forester whom you dropped off in downtown Chicago. This is where a deeper understanding comes into play.

The second level deals more with paying constant attention to specific directional input that is continually processed in relation to one's activity. Knowing the cardinal directions as a constant and keeping track of them as your location changes is very important when it comes to survival. This takes time to learn and will never become a completely subconscious effort even for the best navigators.

I have had the fortune of being instructed in some of the best land navigation training that a person can get. There is hardly ever a time when I couldn't correctly point North. I take pride in the aptitude that I have built up in this arena. Sure, that is great, but I will also humbly say that there have been several times when I found myself utterly confused and awash with that sinking feeling. I'm lost.

During a vacation in Italy, my wife and I spent a day in the beautiful city of Spoleto. We had enjoyed the sights, wandered the streets, and did some shopping. The sun was setting and the time limit for our parking was soon to expire so we needed to head back. Yes, I had a map but when I made the turn that I thought would lead to the car, I suddenly realized that I was dead wrong. I could blame the confusing streets or imperfect map, but the truth is plainly obvious. I was distracted and not paying close enough attention to the directional skills that I have painstakingly honed.

So, we stopped and thought about it. After using the known variables and working them into a framework, we soon got our direction back and found the way to our car. The point here is that even a proficiency with navigation will fail when you lose track of things that you should be paying close attention to in a strange area. It demands cognizant recognition. Fortunately, there are tools and natural elements that can help us to keep our sense of direction grounded.

COMPASS

The traditional instrument contains a magnetized pointer that will indicate a North bearing through its attraction to the Earth's magnetic fields. The origin of the compass is not truly known but there are records about the study of magnetism that date back to the fourth century BC.

Whenever you are trekking into unknown areas, it is a good idea to have a compass. It is easy to find a small compass that can be clipped to a belt-loop or your pack. It doesn't need to be overly expensive as long as the pointer moves evenly, and it gives you a correct reading. Downloading a compass application for your phone or mobile device will also be helpful where you have service. For your main pack, you might want something that is more durable and higher in quality. I use a trusted Cammenga 3H that is still detailed with a fine layer of Afghanistan's persistent dust.

Remember that a compass works off magnetic fields and can, therefore, give a false reading if it is disrupted by certain things. Hold your compass level so that the pointer moves freely. When taking a reading, keep it away from magnets, metal objects, and electronic devices. Standing under power lines or near power stations will also affect it. Hold it out in front of you on an open palm so that you can clearly read the direction.

When you line the N on the compass up with the pointer, you will be facing North. As indicated on the compass, East will be at 90 degrees to your right, South is directly behind you at 180 degrees and West will be at 270 degrees to your left. Knowing

North and facing that way, you can always find the other three if you remember this order.

GPS

The global positioning system is an electronic device that shows a signature of your current position by using a signal from a satellite. It was initially designed for the use of the U.S. military but has now made it into public circulation and is widely used for many applications. For the most part, the technology has become very accurate in the places where you can get a reliable signal. They will also give you a map feature to work with. Any of the many variations can be extremely helpful when you need to find your direction.

For survival and wilderness navigation you will want to get a device that is specific to this type of use. These will be designed to fit requirements that are commonly encountered in the outdoor setting. They are better at picking up a signal in hard to reach places, and you will be able to download more functional maps that will have the necessary information on them. Make sure that you are fully proficient with a GPS before you venture out with it. Plenty of people have gotten lost because they were dependent upon a good device, but they did not know how to utilize it properly.

Make sure that you do research if you want to get a GPS device. The features, capabilities, and price can vary a great deal. There are a few downfalls that you should keep in mind. Lack of good signal can mean that your position is not accurate, or you cannot find it at all. These devices need a power source that can run out or fail when you need it. While most are rather durable, these are still electronics and can be subject to any number of issues that will compromise proper functioning.

Call me old-fashioned, but I will still put my trust into the concrete reliability of a good map and compass any day. When using a GPS in the military we always referenced it with the map and compass as well. GPS is a nice modern companion to the traditional forms of navigation.

Shadow-Tip Method

There are times that you will not have a compass but will still need a reliable indication of direction. Everywhere except the polar regions, the sun will rise in the east and cross the sky to where it sets in the west. This alone will give you a fair estimate of the cardinal directions, but the earth's rotation and the shadows cast by the sun can give you a more accurate reading.

1. Find a mostly level spot in the sun and a straight stick that is about waist-high. Clear away any brush or debris so that your stick can cast an unobstructed shadow.

2. Poke the stick into the ground so that it stands upright vertically.

3. Make a mark or place a stone at the tip of the shadow which is cast by the stick.

4. Wait for fifteen minutes or until the shadow moves about a hand width away from the mark.

5. Mark the tip of the shadow's new position.

6. Draw an arm-length line from the first mark so that it connects the two marks and extends past the second. This is the east/west line.

7. Stand with your left foot on the first mark and the other foot at the end of your line.

If you are in the northern hemisphere, you will be facing north. If you are in the southern hemisphere, this same positioning will have you facing south. If you lay the stick across the east/west line to make a perpendicular it will give you an accurate north/south line.

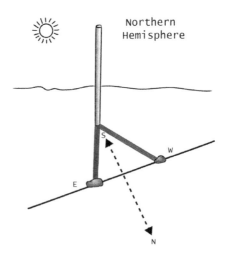

Watch Method

The description will show you how to do this if you have an analog watch with an hour and minute hand. If you have a digital watch, you will need to draw a standard clock on a flat piece of ground. Position the drawn clock in accordance with the description and mark the hands to correspond with the actual time. The steps will differ somewhat depending on which hemisphere you are in. This method is less accurate when you are closer to the equator.

Northern Hemisphere

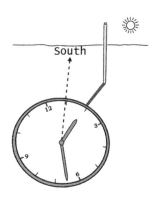

1. Poke a stick in the ground so that it casts a clear shadow.

2. Place your watch on the ground so that the hour hand is lined up with the shadow.

3. Bisect the distance between the hour hand and the twelve o'clock position, then draw a line on the ground to indicate this position.

4. This will be your north/south line and you will be facing south.

Southern Hemisphere

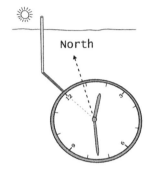

1. Poke a stick in the ground so that it casts a clear shadow.

2. Place your watch on the ground so that the twelve o'clock position is lined up with the shadow.

3. Bisect the distance between the twelve o'clock position and the hour hand and then draw a line on the ground to indicate this position.

4. This will be your north/south line and you will be facing north.

Note: If your watch is set for daylight savings time, you will need to adjust it to factor this out.

STARS

On a clear night, it is possible to find your direction by using the stars. This is one of the oldest and most reliable forms of navigation. In the northern hemisphere, you will need to look for Polaris (North Star). From our position, all other stars appear to revolve around this star as it holds a constant position.

Polaris is not the brightest star in the sky so the easiest way to find it is by using two brighter and more evident constellations.

It is positioned between the seven stars of Ursa Major (Big Dipper) and the five stars that make the constellation Cassiopeia. Remember that these constellations will rotate and move depending upon the season, but Polaris will always remain between them.

Cassiopeia looks like zigzag or lopsided W and a direct line from the center star points to Polaris. Ursa Major looks like a soup ladle and a line that extends from the last two stars in the ladle will point to Polaris. Even if one of the constellations is obscured by clouds, you should be able to have a good indication of where to find the North Star.

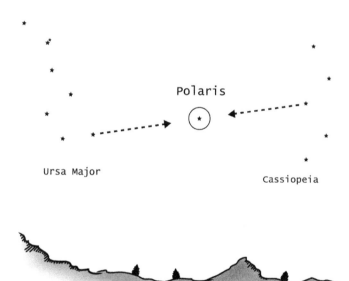

In the southern hemisphere you will need to locate a constellation called the Southern Cross. This will give you an approximate position of south, but it is less accurate than Polaris which cannot be seen when you are south of the Equator. This constellation is made up of four bright stars that look like a tilted cross. The two stars that form the long axis are called the pointers. Draw an imaginary line that extends through the bottom of the cross as if to lengthen the pole of the cross. The line will be five times the distance between the pointers. The end of it will show you the position of south.

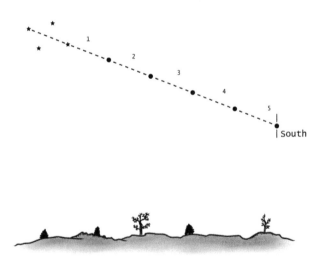

When using the stars to navigate you may not be able to see well enough to move at that time and it may be advisable to wait until daylight. This will mean that you will need to use a stick or line on the ground to make your north/south line. When you can see more clearly, pick out a major feature on the horizon that lines up with the direction that you need to travel and set a course for that point.

Obtaining your direction by use of the sun and stars is nowhere near the accuracy of a compass but in a survival situation, having a general heading is normally good enough. In difficult terrain, it will be important to keep track of direction changes and you may need to verify your heading numerous times. Make good use of easily identifiable land features.

MAP

A map can be a game changer if you have the foresight to prepare yourself. Your emergency backpack at the house should be equipped with a detailed map of your area and a larger map that covers your state or country. If you are close to a border, you will want neighboring maps as well. It is smart to have a map of the local area that you regularly travel in your vehicles. Stash it with the other gear and it can be taken with you if you need to move out on foot. Any time that you are out in an unfamiliar area it is critical to take a map with you and keep track of your location on it.

Most national parks, nature preserves, and tourist places will have a visitor center that will provide an area map for you to use. Good city maps are easy to find but GPS maps will probably be the first choice in these places where reception is reliable. You will likely need to search the internet for maps of more remote areas where you may be hunting, fishing, or engaging in outdoor sports. It will only take a moment to print these before leaving and could end up being a lifesaver.

There are certain things that you will need to look for when picking a map. A map's scale refers to the relationship between the measurements on the map and that of actual distance on the ground. The important thing is to have a map that is detailed enough to provide the information that you need. If you are hiking a trail on the north rim of the Grand Canyon you would not want a map of America or even a state map. The scale will also help you understand distances and make decisions based on facts. That river on the map might look close enough to reach in twenty minutes but the scale can tell you that it is actually much farther than you thought.

It is also important to check the map key. This is where you will find a description of the symbols that are found on that particular map. Many of these symbols are universal but they can vary, so make sure that you know what you are looking at. Get a map that identifies the things that will be pertinent to what you are doing. Campsites, logging roads, boat landings, ski trails, and scenic places name just a few of the things that you may want to look for. All these things can be used when trying to verify location. Spotting a radio tower on a hilltop, train tracks, or a small lake in the distance can help to correlate one's position.

The map compass is another thing that should be present. This shows you how to find North on the map so that you can compare it to reality. Sometimes it will show all four cardinal directions, but it is often represented by an arrow pointing to an N for north. If you are given a map or print one that does not have north identified, ask that person or figure it out ahead of time. Then, draw it in place and use it. To set the map, you will align North on the map with North on the compass or what you have discerned to be north. When you are moving in a different direction it will be less confusing if you turn the map so that it continues to point north.

There are different types of maps that can be considered when making a selection. Most of us are familiar with general reference maps. They show landforms, boundaries, bodies of water, cities, and so forth. Road maps are just as common. Maps can show climate, history, resources and many other themes. Topographical maps use lines to indicate incremental elevation changes that will give you an accurate depiction of the land itself.

Topographical maps are usually the best choice for going into wilderness areas. Most of them will also mark the standard symbols from the key but in vast areas referencing a hilltop or valley may be the only way to discern your location. They are also the best for deciding your course of movement. A direct route on a regular map might lead you to an impassable ravine. Often, a straight heading through the natural landscape is not the best one and a topographical map will help you to figure that out.

The map that you pick should be easy for you to understand. It will have the things that you need to use. If you find a good map which is missing some information that you want, the map can be modified by transferring information onto it. Be sure that you can interpret the different features of the map. As mentioned before, if you find yourself without a map, do whatever you can to make one.

MAGNETIC VARIATION

This can be slightly confusing, but it is good to note that there are some variations in what we understand to be north. A compass will point you at Magnetic North which can vary slightly because of fractional changes in the earth's magnetic field. The North Pole holds a fixed location at the earth's axis point and is closely aligned with Polaris. This is known as True North. There is also a Grid North which is represented by the gridlines on a map and it actually has a very small difference from True North. For survival navigation, the Grid North and True North variance can basically be ignored.

Magnetic variation between a compass and the Grid North that you see on a map will change slightly, depending upon where you are located on the earth. In some places, they will align almost perfectly and with others, the difference will be more drastic. I may be scrutinized for this, but for most wilderness navigation, this variance is not an extremely big deal. Calculating magnetic variance is more important when you are trying to find a very specific point or crossing vast distances.

For military navigation training, we had to cover long distances in the wilderness and find a precise point marked by a numbered post. If you are off by a few degrees in this situation, you will miss your mark. In a functional application, we would be expected to do the same thing when accurately moving to the location of an enemy target. Precision is critical here but the chances that you will need to navigate at such a level are slight.

Often, in wilderness survival, it is important for you to follow a general heading. This heading will keep you from wandering indiscriminately. It will help you to make your way to larger identifiable features that will keep you on track. Don't get bogged down and halt movement because you are unable to calculate the variance between your compass and the North Star or even Grid North on your map. If you only have one North indicator, that is just fine.

So, now that I have gotten myself in trouble with all the great navigators, I will say that, if you have what you need and are able to figure out the magnetic variance, it will not hurt to do so. If the degree of variation is printed on the map, you can use that information to calculate the difference on your compass. The variation should be subtracted from the bearing on your compass before relating it to the map. Conversely, the variation should be added to your map bearing before relating it to your compass.

TERRAIN FEATURES AND TOPOGRAPHY

There are not a lot of places where you will find that the lay of the land is completely flat. Knowing how to identify these features has many uses. Knowing how to navigate by relating these features to a topographical map will give you an immeasurable advantage. The face of the land often follows patterns that will reveal helpful information about your surroundings once you learn to read them.

The terrain features and changes in elevation are shown on a topographical map with contours. These are lines on the map that connect points of equal elevation. This means that if you follow one line, it will represent a specific elevation in that area. The line that is next to it will either be lesser or greater in elevation.

The space between these lines is called the contour interval and shows the distance that you would need to travel before reaching the next contour line. The distance of the contour interval will be found in the margin and can change with each map. The spacing of the interval depicts incline. If the spacing is very close, it will be a steep incline. When they are widely spaced, it means that the incline is gradual.

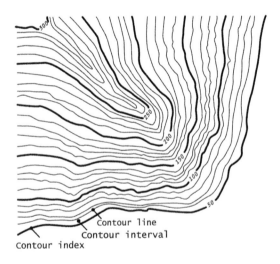

Every fifth line on a topographical map is labeled with a number to show the elevation. These are index contours and the specific reference data that they provide makes the map easier to read. Most of the time they are darker or slightly wider than the regular contours. To figure out the elevation of the unmarked contour lines, add or subtract the contour interval.

The topographical lines on the map will form representations of the features that shape the landscape Hill, ridge, valley, saddle, and depression are the five major features. The minor terrain features are draw, spur, and cliff.

HILL

A hill is an area of high ground where the elevation slopes downward in all directions. This also applies to a mountain which you can think of as an oversized hill. A hill can be a great vantage point when you need to get a good look at the surrounding area. These are also good places to signal for rescuers.

RIDGE

This is a line of high ground that spreads out. The top of the ridge will often have differing points of elevation but the ground on either side of the ridge will always be a lower elevation than the crest of the ridge. Ridges normally have less vegetation because of the water runoff. This makes traveling along them a good choice because of visibility and ease of movement. Areas between the highest points of a ridge are good places to shelter. Select a spot that is on the sunny side and protected from the wind but clear of the runoff zones.

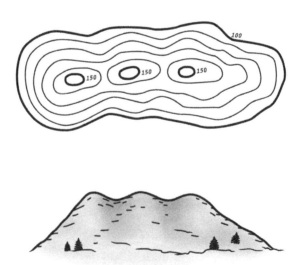

VALLEY

Valleys are places of low ground that will be bordered on the sides by ground that slopes upward in elevation and away from the valley bottom. Contrary to common belief, these terrain features are not limited to low elevations and can even be found high in the mountains if they fit the description above.

They do not always contain streams and rivers, but gravity does naturally cause rainfall to drain here and it is a good place to look for water. Vegetation and animal activity will be denser in the valleys, so it is generally a good place to look for food and building materials as well. Due to the moisture, insect life, and thick plant growth, valley bottoms are normally avoided when it comes to traveling and shelter building.

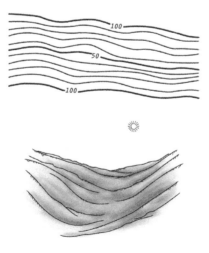

SADDLE

This feature is regularly described as the dip between higher points along the crest of a ridge. Sometimes the crest of a ridge will hold a level elevation that dips in one area to form a saddle. It can also be the low point of two connected hilltops. When you need to travel over a ridge or hilltop, moving through the saddle can be a better choice. They are often not as steep, and it will decrease the amount of elevation that you will need to climb. This will save time and energy and make the actual distance that you need to travel shorter.

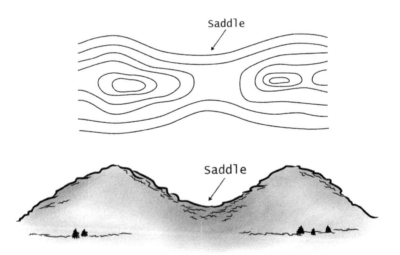

DEPRESSION

This is a hole in the ground or a low point that has higher ground which surrounds it on all sides. Sometimes, on the map a depression will have inward pointing tick marks on the contour lines that surround it.

Some depressions are small, and others take up vast areas. They can sometimes be hard to get into or through, but it might be of interest when you are looking for water or shelter from a tornado.

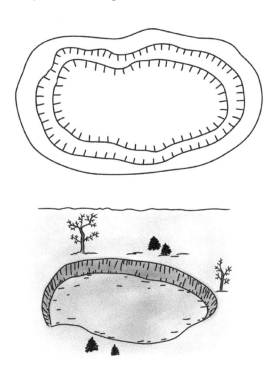

DRAW

A draw is usually a sloped area where runoff or a stream flows down the side of a ridge or hill. It is similar to a valley, but it is smaller and will seldom have a level bottom like a valley. They are caused by erosion and are prone to flash flooding and loose ground which makes them dangerous places for travel and shelter. On the map they can be identified by a V shape in the contour line where the tip of the V points to higher elevation.

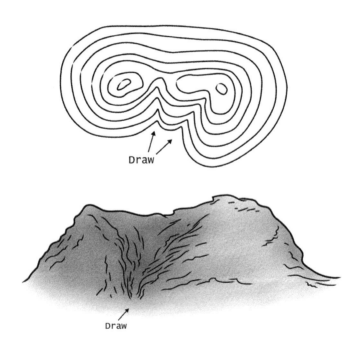

SPUR

The spur is basically the opposite counterpart of the draw. A spur will almost always be seen with a draw on each side of it. They form the higher ground on the sloping sides of ridges and hills. When you need to get over the larger terrain features that spurs form on, traveling up and down a spur is commonly viewed as a wise course.

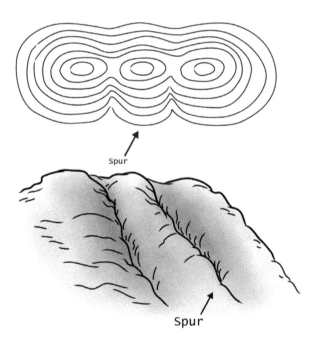

Spur

Spur

CLIFF

This steep and near-vertical slope is easily recognizable. A large cliff will likely be shown on the map by a series of very close or almost touching contour lines that indicate the drastic elevation change. Smaller cliffs will often have a contour line with tick marks that extend downward. It is best to avoid cliffs when traveling. They are dangerous places which are prone to falling rock and landslides. Large cliffs might just be impassable boundaries. To shelter here might offer protection but will also include risk. Use caution when dealing with these terrain features.

ORIENTEERING

Now that we have talked about finding direction, maps, and reading terrain, let's discuss how to make good use of that information when finding our way through the wilderness. The data that you will need to work with can be used in alternate manners. These different ways of navigating are individually important but should all be used in conjunction. They all work together to complete a solid basis of reasoning that will tell you where you are and how to get where you are going.

Recently, people have taken interest in orienteering as an outdoor sport and competitions are held in many locations. In short, competitors are given a compass and map with predetermined points that they need to find in the fastest time possible. For survival purposes, this is simply using a direction to make a heading that will get you to a known point.

In the worst case, you will not have a map, compass, or even a known point to call your destination. None of these things matter. You can still make observations and use the information that you know to make a rudimentary map that can be improved as you go. You still have the alternate methods of finding your direction. You can use logic to make an educated decision about the best heading that you should take. Now, move out confidently and follow that heading as best you can.

It is good to mention one thing that can affect the heading that you are following: drift. We all have one leg that is stronger, one leg that is slightly shorter and an imperfect equilibrium. Our brain also has the natural tendency to direct us around obstacles like trees and on the same side every time. All these things compile incrementally and can send you off course.

To combat drift, it is important to pick out those features in the distance that you can move directly to without compromising your heading. Check the compass or alternate method of direction frequently to have solid confirmation that you are still correct. When there are obstructions in your path, alternate the sides which you take to go around them.

DEAD RECKONING

This is a method of calculating current position by factoring speed, travel time, and distance covered. These things are referenced against your last known location. This can be very helpful in places where visibility is limited by things like fog, dense vegetation, and darkness. It is also useful in featureless landscapes such as desert, tundra, and open plains.

Let's say that you left point A at 0900 hrs on a due south heading. At walking speed, you covered about five kilometers and it is now 1000 hrs. This information can be used to give you an approximate location of your current position at point B. Most of the time this will not be an exact science. If you have the equipment to make it so, then you probably also know precisely where you are and don't need to worry about it.

In the military, we used something called pace count to refine the accuracy of our dead reckoning. This is just a matter of learning how many steps it takes for you to cover 100m. Figure this out ahead of time by walking the measured distance and getting your pace count. It is best to do this on fairly even ground in the wilderness and repeat the process to get a good average. As rangers, we were expected to know our walking and jogging pace count each for movements unencumbered, with a light load and with a heavy load.

Once you know your pace count, keep track of it with Ranger Beads or by transferring small stones from one pocket to another. For each 100m count you will transfer one stone and after ten stones you have moved one kilometer. Cut a notch in a stick to keep track of kilometers covered.

Your pace count will change when moving over difficult terrain or through dense vegetation. Elevation changes will also affect your pace count. Remember that distance covered can be deceiving when you are looking at a map. Your pace count might tell you that you moved 400m up a hill but on the map, elevation is not measured by the scale distance and it could show that you only covered 200m in actual distance.

TERRAIN ASSOCIATION

This is almost always the preferred method of navigation when you can make good use of it. By using the features that you identify in the landscape, you can match them to a topographical map when trying to find your location. Terrain association will allow you to choose between a direct route or one that intelligently follows the landscape. Good terrain association will take less time than the calculation of dead reckoning and is often more forgiving of your mistakes.

Even without a map, you will still be able to use the things that you know about the terrain features to avoid moving through difficult areas. The features will also be used to keep track of progress and provide visual specifics to reference direction. Make good observations of the landscape and let them show you the easiest way to traverse the ground that you need to cover. One of the most important things about terrain association is how it can help to find the smartest way to reach your destination.

DIRT TIME

The hands-on training for navigation is rather straightforward. To a certain degree, we all do some of these things instinctually as we memorize details of the area that we live in. The prevalence of technology and navigational devices has familiarized much of the population with following a set route on a digital map. Now, you will need to apply the things that you already know to what was learned in this chapter.

Set a goal to get yourself a good compass. Something inexpensive is fine at first, but eventually, having a quality instrument will be ideal. Once you get something better, the cheap model can be the backup for your car. Get familiar with your compass and start to carry it around with you. It doesn't matter where you are going at first. Just get comfortable keeping track of your direction and noticing the natural indicators which will verify that direction.

Learn to construct and use the alternate methods of determining direction. The sun and stars are constant elements that can equip you with direction when you are without advanced tools. Anything which can assist you but doesn't need to be carried is highly regarded in the survival world.

Find yourself some good quality maps of the surrounding area and become adept at understanding the information on them. Laminate them if you like and stow copies in your emergency packs. Now, take your compass and use it in conjunction with the map. Start with something easy and progress to a hike through somewhere that has different features that you can navigate to. If you are struggling with this skill, make sure that the area you select is surrounded with roads or has clear backstops that you will come across if you become disoriented.

As your ability to set a course and follow direction improves, you will need to learn your pace count and keep track of distance. Focus on a count that factors in a light pack. You should be carrying this anyway if you learned anything from the previous chapters. At this point, you will put everything together to work on getting better at dead reckoning. Make note of the difference in distance covered when relating between elevation and scale distance on the map.

While practicing these other skills you, will incorporate what you learned about terrain association. Identify the different features with the map and on the ground. You will start to take knowledge from the landscape that can be used to your advantage. Flow with the features of the terrain and move more easily through it. Get better at following a route that is more intelligent and perhaps less direct.

Once you become confident, practice without the modern tools. Select an area that you are only slightly familiar with but will not become lost in. Find your direction by alternate means. Make your own map as you move through this area. Continue to pay attention to your direction and verify it periodically. At this point, you may want to find out if there are any orienteering clubs or events in your area. This will be a fun way to practice a valuable skill.

There are many applications to these tasks and often they can be improved on a regular basis. Remember that as you work on these abilities, you will encounter frustration and disorientation. It happens to everyone. Don't second guess the fundamentals. Stay focused and work through it. Always pay attention to your navigational intuition and it will help you find your way.

FIRST AID

"HEALING IS A MATTER OF TIME, BUT IT IS SOMETIMES ALSO A MATTER OF OPPORTUNITY."

—HIPPOCRATES OF KOS

The situations that lead us into the realm of survival are often associated with risk, danger, and the prospect of dealing with physical complications. At times, you will be able to treat the ailment and let healing complete the equation. Occasionally there will be injuries that you can only partially treat and lend the advantage of time to a problem that requires professional attention. Sadly, you may also be faced with things which are out of your control or beyond your abilities. Harsh as it may be, that is just the way of things.

You need to understand that these are simply the facts and you cannot allow them to prevent you from carrying on. War made this lesson painstakingly clear to me. Minor medical issues are commonplace, so you can easily treat them and move on. This is no big deal, but the bad days do come.

We had nasty battles where soldiers were seriously injured. Sometimes men got patched up, and we kept fighting until it could be dealt with later. Worse cases needed to have severe bleeding stopped so that we could carry the soldiers to safety and immediate attention before they could bleed out. Unfortunately, there were also heroes who paid the ultimate price and no amount of help that we gave them could have changed the outcome.

I hope that you are never faced with the tragedy of war, but the truth is that there are many instances when you can be placed into the path of very similar horrors. Car accidents and natural disasters can produce very real injuries. A spill from the stove can cause severe burns. A child can easily choke from a bite of food or something that shouldn't even be eaten. Falls often result in broken bones. There are too many accidents that can happen and will demand rapid attention. It only makes sense to possess some medical knowledge. In the wilderness or places where you are away from professional help, this necessity is compounded.

To equip yourself for these situations, having basic medical knowledge is the most important factor. Something learned is ideal but many times it can also be referenced data that provides guidance. Use the knowledge to reinforce your composure so that you can act level-headed.

Available medical supplies are also of crucial significance. Certain locations will have these on hand, you may have had the foresight to bring them or it could be something improvised. One time, at the lake, my son broke his arm and I had to make a splint with newspaper and a sling from a towel. It worked fine to restrict movement until we got to the doctor. This is possible for many things, but some items cannot be supplemented. It is always better to be prepared.

MEDICAL KIT

You will want to have medical supplies prepared ahead of time whenever possible. Your kits should be staged in a system of progression which similarly follows that of your other survival equipment. The first stage should focus on prevention. Seriously think about what you are doing and have the things that will mitigate problematic situations. These are not parts of the basic med-kit, but they will keep you from digging into it.

Many injuries are related to natural elements. When dealing with the sun, have plenty of water, sunblock, and clothes that will shield you from it. If you are in poisonous snake territory, wear high boots and bring a snakebite kit. Wear thick protective clothing when you will be out in the cold. Jogging shoes and cotton socks will do you little good when trudging through the snow.

Prevention also includes treating dangerous things as such and acting intelligently. Don't walk on thin ice, so to speak. Think it through and use caution when dealing with things like fire, cold water, sharp objects, and places where you could fall and break something. Accidents do happen but often you can look at the scenario afterward and find that it did not have to.

TRAVEL KIT

This can be looked at in two stages. If you regularly carry a purse, briefcase, or backpack it should have a few simple things in it. If you have personal needs like medication or things for response to allergic reaction, that is foremost. After that, it is good to have a couple of small bandages, aspirin or ibuprofen, alcohol swabs, antiseptic cream, and two safety pins. You may want a few other things, but this kit should be compact and focus on one-time or two-time usage. Keep everything in a small sealable plastic bag and replace items as you use them.

The next stage applies to the occasions that you are doing outdoor activities and excursions. It should be kept with your other basic survival items in a small pack. You will also want to have a similar kit that is kept in each of your cars, recreational vehicles, and large survival packs at home. This kit will be more comprehensive and able to assist in a greater amount of circumstances. Keep this kit focused on covering two-time to four-time usage. All the creams and swabs can be found in individual travel-sized packets. Expect it to be about the size of a brick. Get a good plastic container with a waterproof lid to store the listed items.

- Quick reference medical guide
- Personal needs items
- Assorted bandages (small, medium, large, fingertip, and butterfly)
- Blister pads/Moleskin
- Gauze roll bandage
- Elastic bandage
- Cravat bandage/triangle bandage
- Gauze pads
- Cotton balls
- Medical tape
- Blood clotting agent
- Burn gel packets
- Burn gel dressing
- Alcohol swabs
- Antibacterial cream
- Sting cream
- Rash cream
- Rehydration salts
- Sunblock
- Mylar blanket
- Latex gloves
- Safety pins
- Tweezers
- Fingernail clippers
- Small scissors
- 2-5 meters of 550 cord
- Pain/anti-inflammatory tablets

Note: Aspirin and ibuprofen will thin blood, so if someone is bleeding, Tylenol (acetaminophen) is a better alternative. Understand the hazards of any medication and make sure that it is used in accordance with its intended use. Just because it is safe for you does not mean that someone you are assisting will not have an adverse reaction.

MEDICAL BAG

This kit will pertain mostly to household use but will also be ready if you need to evacuate your home for any reason. It will hold the bulk of your medical equipment and be able to sustain your medical needs for an extended period of time. Other than the few items that can be used repeatedly, greater quantities of the items listed above will make up a large portion of this bag. If you need to take this bag with you, there should be some available space for important things from the medicine cabinet or elsewhere. Everything must be bagged/waterproofed and should fit into a standard backpack or small gym bag when you are finished. Below is a list of additional items to include.

- Cold packs
- Eye flush
- Eye bandage
- Sutures
- Soap
- Antihistamine medication
- Antidiarrheal medication
- Medical scissors
- Braces (ankle, knee, wrist…)
- Sling
- Ready to use splints
- Headlamp

PROVIDING AID

Much of the remainder will be put into a format which can allow you to quickly reference ailments and move on to treating them. At times, you may need to treat yourself, but you will more commonly be helping those around you. Sometimes you will know exactly what they need and will be able to proceed directly, but there is also a chance that you will come across an accident and do not know what kind of aid that person needs.

ASSESS THE SITUATION

1. No matter the severity of the situation, DO NOT PANIC. Calm your breathing and think clearly.

2. When possible, and casualties do not need immediate aid, call for emergency responders.

3. Make sure that the scene is safe for you and other aid workers.

4. Find out how many casualties there are and use your senses to provide clues about what happened and the kinds of injuries you may be dealing with.

5. Enlist the aid of anyone on the scene who is able to help. First, have them call or go for help if they do not need to assist you with casualties who need immediate aid.

6. Move any casualties that need to get away from immediate danger but do not put yourself in harm's way. (Don't move someone if there isn't a need)

7. Evaluate the casualties and the injuries that they have so that you can prioritize those who need more urgent care. (Those who are not breathing will require treatment first. Anyone missing limbs or with severe arterial bleeding will also need immediate aid)

8. Stay confident and boost the morale of the survivors by offering reassurance and letting them know that you are there to help.

EVALUATE CASUALTIES

1. Check for responsiveness.

    A. In a loud but calm voice, ask if they are all right.

    B. Tap the casualty on the shoulder or gently shake them.

    C. If there is no response, proceed directly to step two.

    D. If they are responsive, ask what is wrong and where there is pain.

    E. If they are responsive but show signs of choking, (the universal sign for choking is hands clutched to the throat) proceed to Choking/Breathing Obstruction Treatment (p. 250).

2. Check for breathing.

    A. Open the airway. With the person laying on their back, tilt the head back slightly to lift the chin.

    B. Look for a rising and falling motion of the chest.

C. Place your ear close to their mouth and nose and listen for breathing.

D. Feel for breathing by positioning your cheek or the back of your hand next to the casualty's mouth and nose. (Occasional gasping sounds do not equate breathing.)

E. Examine the airway for blockage and remove any obstructions.

F. If they are not breathing, proceed to CPR/ Resuscitation Treatment (p. 247).

3. Check for bleeding.

A. Look for pooled blood, blood-soaked clothes, or spurting blood.

B. Check for an entry and exit point to the wound.

C. If bleeding is identified, proceed to Bleeding Wounds Treatment (p. 253).

4. Check for shock.

A. Look for any of the following symptoms and/or signs that identify the presence of shock.

a. Clammy or sweaty cool skin.
b. Pale tone to the skin.
c. Bleeding and loss of blood.
d. Confused state.
e. Nervousness or restless demeanor.
f. Thirst.

g. Fast or uncontrolled breathing.

h. Vomiting and/or nausea.

i. Blotchy or blue coloration to the skin near the mouth.

B. If any of the symptoms or signs are identified, proceed to Shock Treatment (p. 256).

5. Check for fractures.

A. Check for the following symptoms and signs of back, spine, and neck injury.

a. Indication of pain, pressure, or soreness in the neck or back area.

b. Bruising, cuts, or abrasions in the neck or back area.

c. The casualty is unable to move due to numbness or paralysis. (Touch their arms and legs to see if they can feel it and ask if they are able to move)

d. Look for unusual limb or body position.

B. If they are suspected of having a neck, back, or spine injury, immobilize them by doing the following steps:

a. Ask them to refrain from movement.

b. For a back or spine injury, carefully tuck padding at each side of the back's natural arch to give support.

c. For neck injury, carefully tuck padding under the neck and place something stable on each side of the head to keep it from turning.

    d. These injuries will require that the body remains immobilized until professional medical attention can be given.

    e. In remote areas where movement is necessary, a stretcher will need to be constructed.

C. Check the body and limbs for fractures.

    a. Check for open fractures by looking for bones protruding through the skin, bleeding, and deformities.

    b. Check for closed fractures by looking for deformity, swelling, discoloration, and unnatural body position.

D. If indications of a fracture are present, then proceed to Fracture/Broken Bone Treatment (p. 257).

6. Check for burns.

A. Inspect the casualty for singed clothing and areas where the skin is charred, blistered, or reddened.

B. If burns are evident, proceed to Burn Treatment (p. 260).

7. Check for head injury.

A. Look for the following symptoms and signs that indicate head injury.

    a. Dizziness

    b. Confusion

    c. Headache

d. Unequal pupils

e. Loss of consciousness

f. Slurred speech

g. Memory loss

h. Sleepiness

i. Fluid from the mouth, ears, nose or injury site.

j. Loss of balance

k. Vomiting

l. Twitching or convulsions

m. Paralysis

B. If there is evidence that indicates a head injury, restrict movement and monitor the casualty for signs that would require treatment of CPR/Resuscitation (p. 247) or treatment for Shock (p. 256).

8. Proceed to treat other casualties in the order of priority.

9. Monitor treated casualties and provide additional aid as needed.

10. Continue to seek professional assistance without interrupting necessary treatment.

CPR/RESUSCITATION TREATMENT

Steps for CPR from the
American Red Cross standards of 2019 (redcross.org)

ADULT

1. If there is someone there to help, send them to get an AED/defibrillator (if available) otherwise begin to administer aid.

2. Push hard, push fast. Place your hands, one on top of the other, in the middle of the chest. Use your body weight to help you deliver compressions that are at least two inches deep and delivered at a rate of at least 100 compressions per minute.

3. Deliver rescue breaths. With the person's head tilted back slightly and the chin lifted, pinch the nose shut and place your mouth over the person's mouth to make a complete seal. Blow into the person's mouth to make the chest rise. Deliver two rescue breaths, then continue compressions.

Note: If the chest does not rise with the initial rescue breath, re-tilt the head before delivering the second breath. If the chest doesn't rise with the second breath, the person may be choking. After each subsequent set of 30 chest compressions, and before attempting breaths, look for blockage in the airway and, if seen, remove it.

4. Continue CPR steps. Keep performing cycles of chest compressions and rescue breathing until the person exhibits signs of life, an AED becomes available, or an EMS or trained medical responder arrives at the scene.

Note: End the cycles if the scene becomes unsafe or you cannot continue performing CPR due to exhaustion.

CPR/RESUSCITATION FOR CHILD/INFANT

1. Deliver two rescue breaths if the child or infant isn't breathing. With the head tilted back slightly and the chin lifted, pinch the child's nose shut, make a complete seal by placing your mouth over the child's mouth. Now, deliver two rescue breaths.

Note: For small infants, use your mouth to make a complete seal over the mouth and nose, then blow in for one second to make the chest clearly rise. Now, deliver two rescue breaths.

2. Begin CPR. If the child or infant is unresponsive to the rescue breaths, begin CPR.

3. Kneel beside the child or infant.

4. Push hard, push fast.

   A. For children, place the heel of one hand on the center of the chest, then place the heel of the other hand on top of the first hand and lace your fingers together. Deliver 30 quick compressions that are each about two inches deep.

    B.   For infants, use two fingers to deliver 30 quick compressions that are each about 1.5 inches deep.

5.   Give two rescue breaths (see instructions above).

6.   Keep going. Continue the child or infant CPR steps until you see obvious signs of life, an AED becomes available, or an EMS or trained medical responder arrives at the scene.

Note: End the cycles if the scene becomes unsafe or you cannot continue performing CPR due to exhaustion.

CHOKING/BREATHING OBSTRUCTION TREATMENT

Steps to treat choking from Mayo Foundation for Medical Education and Research 2019 (mayoclinic.org)

ADULT OR CHILD

1. If you encounter a conscious, choking individual that is coughing, encourage continued coughing. If the victim is unable to cough, speak, or breathe, complete the following steps.

2. Send someone to call emergency responders.

3. Give five back blows. Stand to the side and just behind a choking adult. For a child, kneel behind. Place one arm across the person's chest for support. Bend the person over at the waist so that the upper body is parallel with the ground. Deliver five separate back blows between the person's shoulder blades with the heel of your hand.

4. Give five abdominal thrusts.

    A. Stand behind the person. Place one foot slightly in front of the other for balance. Wrap your arms around the waist. Tip the person forward slightly. If a child is choking, kneel behind the child.

    B. Make a fist with one hand. Position it slightly above the person's navel. For a pregnant or obese person, place your hands at the base of the breastbone, just above the joining of the lowest ribs.

   C. Grasp the fist with the other hand. Press hard into the abdomen with a quick, upward thrust—as if trying to lift the person up.

5. Alternate between five blows and five thrusts until the blockage is dislodged.

6. If the person loses consciousness, proceed to CPR/ Resuscitation Treatment (p. 247).

CHOKING/BREATHING OBSTRUCTION OF INFANT UNDER AGE ONE.

1. Assume a seated position and hold the infant face down on your forearm, which is resting on your thigh. Support the infant's head and neck with your hand and place the head lower than the trunk.

2. Thump the infant gently but firmly five times in the middle of the back using the heel of your hand. The combination of gravity and the back blows should release the blocking object. Keep your fingers pointed up to avoid hitting the infant in the back of the head.

3. Turn the infant face up on your forearm, resting on your thigh with the head lower than the trunk if the infant still isn't breathing. Using two fingers placed at the center of the infant's breastbone, give five quick chest compressions. Press down about 1.5 inches, and let the chest rise again in between each compression.

4. Repeat the back blows and chest thrusts if breathing doesn't resume. Call for emergency help.

5. If one of these techniques opens the airway but the infant does not resume breathing, proceed to CPR/Resuscitation for Infant (p. 248).

Note: If the infant is older than age one and conscious, give abdominal thrusts only. Be careful not to use too much force to avoid damaging ribs or internal organs.

CHOKING/BREATHING OBSTRUCTION FOR SELF

1. Call emergency responders immediately. You may not be able to talk but help should respond to the call.

2. Place a fist slightly above your navel.

3. Grasp your fist with the other hand and bend over a hard surface like a countertop or chair.

4. Shove your fist inward and upward.

BLEEDING WOUND TREATMENT

1. Wash hands and/or put on surgical gloves.

2. Clean the wound and remove debris that moves freely. Do not remove large debris that is lodged in the wound.

3. If available, apply clotting agent as directed for severe bleeding.

4. Apply direct pressure to the wound or cut by using gauze or a clean piece of cloth to prevent blood loss. If nothing is available to cover the wound, just apply pressure with your hand. Depending upon the severity of the wound, clotting should take place between five and 15 minutes. If the injured person is able, have them apply pressure so that you can continue treatment or treat others. Do not put direct pressure onto lodged debris if present.

5. Do not remove the dressing if blood soaks through it. Add more gauze or cloth and continue to apply pressure.

6. If the wound is on an extremity, elevate it above the heart if possible. This will help to slow bleeding.

7. Once the bleeding stops, use tape or strips of cloth to wrap and bandage the injury firmly but not so tight as to restrict normal blood flow.

8. Monitor circulation below the bandage if it is a limb.

9. Keep the wound site clean and change the bandages daily.

10. Watch for signs of infection and blood poisoning.

ARTERIAL BLEEDING (BRIGHT RED SPURTING BLOOD)

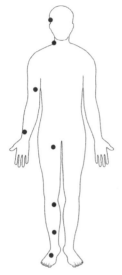

1. Reducing the blood flow is critical.

2. Apply pressure to the main arteries at pressure points where they are close to the bone.

3. Watch the wound and move the location of pressure until the blood slows.

4. If available, apply clotting agent as directed.

5. Cover the wound with gauze or cloth and apply pressure to the wound site as well.

6. The victim should be covered to retain body heat and help to prevent shock.

TOURNIQUET

WARNING: This technique is only used as a last resort when an arm or leg has been completely cut off, or if there is no chance of professional aid coming to treat severe bleeding that will not stop, and the victim is facing death due to extreme blood loss. Partially severed limbs should be treated with arterial pressure and direct pressure to the wound site.

1. A tourniquet should be at least two (5 cm) inches wide. Cravat, cloth or strong pliable material works best.

2. Tourniquet positioning.

   A. Place it over smoothed clothing if possible.

B. Position the tourniquet about two to four (5-10 cm) inches away from the wound but not over the top of a joint. The tourniquet must separate the flow of blood from the wound site.

C. If the wound is on the joint or just below the joint, the tourniquet will be positioned just above the joint.

3. Apply the tourniquet.

A. Tie the cloth around the limb and secure it with a snug half-hitch.

B. Over the half-hitch, place a strong stick, closed pocket knife, lighter, multi-tool or another device that can be used as a windlass. Then, tie it in place with two half-hitches.

C. Twist the windlass around so that the tourniquet begins to tighten. Continue to twist until the bright spurting and major bleeding stops. Some dark blood may continue to seep from the wound.

4. Secure the windlass.

A. Use the ends of the tourniquet or a shoestring to tie the ends of the windlass in place.

B. Make sure that it is fully secured and will not come loose or unwind.

5. Dress and cover the wound with gauze and bandaging.

6. Elevate the wound if possible.

7. Monitor casualty and treat for Shock if necessary (p. 256).

Note: When there is time to do so, record the time that the tourniquet was applied. This will be important information for further treatment by medical professionals.

SHOCK TREATMENT

Untreated shock is dangerous and can actually kill. It should be taken very seriously and treated quickly.

1. Positioning

    A. Lay the person on their back. If it will help them to breathe more easily and keep calm; a reclined sitting position will also work.

    B. If the person does not have an abdominal injury, un-splinted leg fracture or head wound, elevate the legs.

2. Loosen restricting clothing around the waist, neck, and other areas.

3. Protect the casualty from the elements.

    A. In cold weather, keep the person from direct con-tact with the ground. Use a ground cover and a blanket or improvised covering to maintain the core temperature.

    B. In hot weather, provide shade and cover from direct sunlight.

4. Keep the casualty from eating or drinking.

5. Confidently reassure the person that they are being cared for. Help them to remain calm.

6. Keep their head turned to one side to prevent them from choking if vomiting occurs.

7. If the casualty loses consciousness and keeps breathing, place them in the recovery position (p. 263).

8. Monitor for loss of breathing and be prepared to admin-ister CPR (p. 247).

FRACTURE/BROKEN BONE TREATMENT

1. Prepare the casualty.

   A. If they are conscious, reassure them that you are going to help.

   B. Loosen any tight or restricting clothing.

   C. Remove any jewelry from the affected area to prevent injury from swelling. Put jewelry into the individual's pocket.

   D. Do not straighten or try to reposition the fracture into its natural location.

2. Gather splint materials.

   A. Splints are rigid materials that will extend beyond the joints above and below the break. Things like branches, poles, boards, and rolled magazines or newspapers work well if you do not have a professional splint.

   B. Get things to pad the splint. Use clothing, moss, fabric, leafy vegetation, or anything relatively soft.

   C. Find cordage for tying the splint. Use rope, strips of fabric, shoe laces, or anything that can securely bind the splint together. When materials are not available, use clothing to immobilize a fractured arm against the victim's chest or wrap a fractured leg to the person's other leg.

3. For an open fracture, do not attempt to push the bone back into place or under the skin. Apply gauze to stop bleeding and bandage the wound to protect the area.

4. Inspect the limb for circulation problems.

   A. Look for skin discoloration in the skin on the hand or foot of the affected limb.

   B. Press the fingernail or toenail to check if the color returns at a normal rate. Compare to an uninjured limb. Less than two seconds is normal.

   C. Check to see if the limb is colder than an uninjured one.

   D. Ask if there is a feeling of numbness, cold sensation or tingling feeling.

   Blood circulation problems require more urgent attention and will need to be identified when professional assistance is available.

5. Attach the splint

   A. Keep a fractured limb in the position that you find it. The splint is intended to immobilize the area so that further damage is avoided until professional attention can be given.

   B. Put the splinting poles into position on each side of the limb. Make sure that they go past the joints above and below the fractured bone.

   C. Pad the poles by securing cushion that will create space between the splint and parts of the limb. This

is to prevent friction between the hard splint materials and the body. It does not need to be excessive.
Too much padding will cause the splint to be loose
and ineffective.

D. Tie the splints into position above and below the
fracture. Use two overhand knots that are positioned
on the side of the splint that is away from the body.
Be sure to tie it in at least two places on each side
of the fracture. Do not tie splints directly over the
fractured area.

6. Check to make sure that the splint is stable and holds the
fractured area in position. Make any needed adjustments
that will cause the splint to be fully effective.

7. Ensure that there are not any circulation problems
caused by the splint itself.

8. When applicable, attach a sling to further immobilize a
fractured arm or take the weight off a fractured shoulder
blade or collarbone.

A. Use clothing, cravat, poncho, or other material to
make the sling.

B. Position the arm in the sling so that the hand is
higher than the elbow.

C. Tie the sling around the body so that the supporting
pressure is put to the uninjured side.

BURN TREATMENT

Tissue damage in the form of a burn can come from numerous sources. Open flame, scalding, friction, and overexposure to the sun are the most common, but burns can also come from electrocution, freezing metal, and chemicals.

MAJOR BURN

1. Look for signs and symptoms to identify a major burn:

    A. Visibly deep burn that may possibly expose ligament or bone.

    B. Burn that gives the skin a dry and leathery appearance.

    C. Charred patches or burned flesh that is black, white or brown in color.

    D. Burns that are larger than three inches (8 cm) in diameter.

    E. Burns that cover the face, hands, feet, groin area, or a major joint.

2. Remove any belts, jewelry, and loosen restrictive clothing and shoes. Expect rapid swelling of burned areas.

3. Cover the burned area with something cool. Use a burn gel dressing or a cloth/bandage that is moistened with clean water.

4. Refrain from immersing a severe burn in cold water or covering the area in something that is very cold. This can result in major loss of body heat and lead to shock or hypothermia.

5. Clean the area as best that you can but do not try to remove charred clothing or fibers that are stuck to the burn site.

6. Cover the area with a non-stick gauze or a burn gel dressing and bandage the wound to protect the area. Don't use fluffy covering that will stick to the wound, like cotton.

7. If possible, elevate the burned area to a position that is above heart level.

8. Treat minor burns that may be present as well.

9. Monitor the individual for signs and symptoms of shock and be prepared to treat them accordingly.

Major burns will require immediate medical attention.

MINOR BURNS

1. Look for signs and symptoms to identify a minor burn:

   A. Blisters.

   B. Pain and tenderness.

   C. Sunburn or red coloration to the skin.

   D. A burned area that is smaller than three inches (8 cm) in diameter. Minor sunburn can be more widespread but may be severe when the skin is deeply reddened and blistered.

2. Remove jewelry or restrictive clothing from the area. This can be done in conjunction with the cooling of the burn in the next step.

3. Cool the burned area by immersing the burn in cool (not cold) water, holding it under cool running water or applying a burn gel dressing. Cool for at least 10 minutes.

4. Leave blisters intact and take care not to break them. They protect against further chances of infection and cushion the wounded area.

5. Cover the burn with gauze and bandage or wrap it loosely so that you do not put added pressure on the location. A bandage will protect blisters, reduce pain, and keep air from drying the area.

6. Burn cream or lotion with aloe vera can also be used to provide relief and prevent drying but watch for rashes and allergic reaction.

RECOVERY POSITION

An unconscious person with normal breathing and no serious head or spinal injury should be placed in the recovery position to prevent choking on blood, vomit, or the tongue. The least injured side of the body should have the leg straight and the arm extended overhead. The opposite arm will cross over the chest and the other leg will be bent up at the knee and hip. Modify the recovery position if it conflicts with injuries, splints, or bandages.

Carefully roll the person to the fully extended side with the head supported by the arm. Without two or more people, you will have to lay alongside them and use your body to carefully roll them to the face down position. Use clothing or padding to provide support if needed. The face should be to the side with the mouth slightly downward. The person should be partially propped on the bent arm and leg. Keep the back, neck, and head in line.

Hand supports head

Bent leg supports body

DEHYDRATION

Dehydration will take place in any environment and temperature condition.

1. Dehydration signs and symptoms:
   A. Increased thirst.
   B. Lips, mouth, and throat become dry.
   C. Fatigued body, sluggishness, or sleepy feeling.
   D. Decreased urination that has a dark yellow color.
   E. Headache.
   F. Dizziness or light-headed feeling.

DEHYDRATION TREATMENT

1. Regulate a normal body temperature. May require warming or cooling.

2. Loosen or open any clothing that will restrict circulation.

3. Get the person onto a ground cover in a reclined position with the feet elevated.

4. Refrain from eating.

5. Ensure that the person continuously sips cool water throughout the recovery process. A minimum of one liter. If available, add rehydration salts as per the instructions on the packaging.

6. Refrain from strenuous activity.

7. Continue rehydration and recovery until symptoms subside.

HEAT INJURIES

1. Identify the heat-related injury.

    A. Heat Cramps signs and symptoms.

        a. Thirst or parched feeling.

        b. Profuse sweating.

        c. Cramping in the muscles of the legs, arms, and abdominal area.

Proceed to Heat Cramps Treatment (p. 266).

    B. Heat Exhaustion signs and symptoms.

        a. Heavy sweating.

        b. Skin that feels cool and looks pale.

        c. Dizzy or lightheaded sensation.

        d. Headache.

        e. Loss of energy or weakened state.

        f. Loss of appetite.

        g. The presence of heat cramps.

        h. Elevated rate of breathing.

        i. Nausea and possibly vomiting.

        j. Chills or cold sensation.

        k. Tingling in the extremities.

        l. Trouble thinking clearly or confusion.

Proceed to Heat Exhaustion Treatment (p. 267).

C. Heat Stroke signs and symptoms.

    a. Skin that is hot, dry, reddened, and without sweat. These indicate that the body is severely dehydrated.

    b. Dizzy or lightheaded sensation.

    c. Severe headache.

    d. Loss of energy or weakened state.

    e. Nauseous feeling.

    f. Trouble thinking clearly or confusion.

    g. Loss of consciousness.

    h. Rapid breathing and pulse.

    i. Seizures.

Proceed to Heat Stroke Treatment (p. 268).

HEAT CRAMPS TREATMENT

1. Get the person to a cool area with moving air and shade if possible. Improvise some kind of cover or protected area if you must.

2. Loosen or open clothing that is restricting or prevents the body from cooling. Remove shoes and socks.

3. Ensure that the person continuously sips cool water throughout the recovery process. A minimum of one liter. If available, add rehydration salts as per the instructions on the packaging.

4. Continue recovery and rehydration until symptoms subside.

5. Refrain from strenuous activity for at least one day after.

HEAT EXHAUSTION TREATMENT

1. Get the person to a cool area with moving air and shade if possible. Improvise some kind of cover or protected area if you must.

2. Loosen or open clothing that is restricting or prevents the body from cooling. Remove shoes and socks.

3. Slowly pour water onto the person's head and body. Discontinue when body temperature is normal. If water is in short supply, moisten the head and body with a wet rag.

4. Cool the person with fanning.

5. Ensure that the person continuously sips cool water throughout the recovery process. A minimum of two liters. If available, add rehydration salts as per the instructions on the packaging.

6. Elevate the person's legs.

7. Continue recovery and rehydration until symptoms subside.

8. Refrain from strenuous activity for at least one day after.

HEAT STROKE TREATMENT

Heat stroke should be treated as a medical emergency and can result in death without immediate attention. Call for emergency responders if possible.

1. Get the person to a cool area with moving air and shade if possible. Improvise some kind of cover or protected area if you must.

2. Loosen or open clothing that is restricting or prevents the body from cooling. Remove shoes and socks.

3. Slowly pour water onto the person's head and body. Discontinue when body temperature is normal. If water is in short supply, moisten the head and body with a wet rag.

4. Cool the person with fanning.

5. Ensure that the person continuously sips cool water throughout the recovery process. A minimum of four liters over time. If available, add rehydration salts as per the instructions of the packaging.

6. Gently massage the person's arms and legs.

7. Elevate the person's legs.

8. Make sure that the body temperature does not fall below normal. The person may need to be kept warm as recovery progresses.

9. Monitor the person for symptoms that will require treatment for Shock (p. 256) or CPR (p. 247).

10. Continue recovery and rehydration until professional aid can be rendered or symptoms subside. Recovery from heat stroke is a long process. Expect initial recovery to take up to two days, but a full recovery can take months, depending upon the severity.

11. Refrain from strenuous activity until the body regains a normal state.

COLD INJURIES

1. Identify the cold-related injury.

   A. ***Snow Blindness*** signs and symptoms due to exposing the eyes to bright sunlit or reflective landscape for a prolonged time.

      a. Watery eyes.
      b. Reddened eyes.
      c. A scratchy irritated feeling in the eyes.
      d. Headache.
      e. Pain associated with light exposure.

Proceed to Snow Blindness Treatment (p. 273).

   B. ***Chilblain*** signs and symptoms due to prolonged exposure to cold temperatures.

      a. Skin is reddened or even pale white in worse cases.
      b. Area has lost sensation or is numb to pain.
      c. The affected area may have open sores or damage to the tissue.
      d. Light freezing of outer tissue.

Proceed to Chilblain Treatment (p. 274).

   C. ***Frostbite*** signs and symptoms due to drastic cold or extensive exposure to cold temperatures.

Superficial frostbite.

    a. Immediate whitening of the skin after contact with drastic cold or touching a drastically cold object. Often followed by a brief tingling sensation.

    b. Area has lost sensation or is numb to pain.

    c. Redness or ashy color to the skin. Color variation will depend upon the individual's natural skin pigment.

    d. Freezing of tissue.

Proceed to Frostbite Treatment (p. 274).

Deep Frostbite.

    a. Area has become sore and painful.

    b. Area is swollen or tender.

    c. Patches of skin have become waxy and pale.

    d. Appearance of blisters on the affected area.

    e. Affected area is deeply frozen and the skin feels hard and solid to the touch.

Proceed to Frostbite Treatment (p. 274).

Trench foot signs and symptoms due to prolonged exposure to wet conditions and cold temperatures.

    a. Area feels cold.

    b. Area becomes numb.

    c. Progression causes the area to become painful and feel like it is burning.

d. Area takes on a blue or purplish color.

e. Progression causes the area to develop blisters and open sores.

f. The affected area will eventually experience serious bleeding and gangrene if left untreated.

Proceed to Trench Foot Treatment (p. 275).

Hypothermia signs and symptoms due to a large decrease in core body temperature. It does not have to be extremely cold for the effects of hypothermia to set in. Exposure due too inadequate shelter and/or clothing is a major cause. Immersion in cold water or a body that is wet for a prolonged period of time will also cause hypothermia. Anxiety, exhaustion, and injury are other contributing factors.

Mild Hypothermia

a. Fits of uncontrollable shivering.

b. Loss of coordination.

c. Headache.

d. Lethargy and loss of ambition.

e. Slurring of speech.

f. Pale and cold skin.

g. Weak pulse.

Proceed to Hypothermia Treatment (p. 276).

Severe Hypothermia

     a. Delayed response.
     b. Sedated appearance.
     c. Unconsciousness.
     d. Blurred vision and glassy eyes.
     e. Almost no pulse.
     f. Slow and weak breathing.
     g. Skin is frigid.

Proceed to Hypothermia Treatment (p. 276).

SNOW BLINDNESS TREATMENT

1. Get the person into a dark shelter.
2. Blindfold the person with a fabric that blocks all light.
3. Place a cool damp cloth on the person's forehead.
4. Seek medical aid if possible

Vision should fully return over time, but further exposure should be limited by protective eye covering.

CAUTION: Rapid rewarming of chilblain, frostbite, trench foot, and hypothermic injuries is damaging and will be indicated by severe pain. Avoid contact with anything hot or direct heat sources. Do not rub, massage or roughly handle the injured area to avoid additional tissue damage.

CHILBLAIN TREATMENT

1. Slowly rewarm the affected area.

    A. Remove any frozen or wet clothing.

    B. Bandage any open sores.

    C. Use your body heat to rewarm the area by covering with hands, tucking into armpits, or holding in contact with the body core. (Read CAUTION on p. 273.)

    D. Provide a ground cover. Keep the person dry and from direct contact with the cold ground.

    E. Wrap with a blanket and keep sheltered.

2. Treatment for frostbite may be needed.

3. Seek medical aid when possible.

FROSTBITE TREATMENT

1. Slowly rewarm the affected area. Do not rewarm feet if the person will need to walk to medical aid, thawing the area will cause more pain and damage.

    A. Remove any wet or frozen clothing.

    B. Remove jewelry and loosen tight clothing to improve circulation.

    C. Carefully bandage any wounds and cover blisters to prevent popping.

    D. Use your body heat to rewarm the area by covering with hands, tucking into armpits, or holding in contact with the body core. (Read CAUTION on p. 273.)

    E. Provide a ground cover. Keep the person dry and from direct contact with the cold ground.

    F. Wrap with a blanket and keep sheltered.

2. Encourage movement that will not cause damage to the affected areas.

3. Seek medical aid when possible.

4. Use extra care to keep the area from being affected again.

TRENCH FOOT TREATMENT

1. Take time to dry the area thoroughly with warm air. Do not rub or massage. (Read CAUTION on p. 273.)

2. The area will be tender. Carefully bandage and protect any sores or blisters.

3. Elevate the affected area.

4. Keep the area completely dry.

5. Refrain from walking or movement that will damage the area.

6. Seek medical aid if possible.

7. Healing will require the area to be kept dry and rested until healing is complete.

HYPOTHERMIA TREATMENT

1. Call for aid if possible. This is a medical emergency and will require immediate attention.

2. Remove wet clothing, dry the body, and replace with dry garments, starting from the person's core.

3. Provide a ground cover. Keep the person dry and away from direct contact with the cold ground.

4. Hypothermic individuals cannot heat themselves. Use external heat to rewarm. (Read CAUTION on p. 273.)

    A. Provide protection from the elements.

    B. Use sources such as a heater, fire, candle, heated shelter, warm rocks, or a warmed bottle of water.

    C. Use your body heat to give added warmth. Focus warmth to the core area, lower back, neck, armpits, inner thighs, and wrists.

5. Insulate heat with layered clothing and blankets.

6. If conscious, provide the person with warm liquids.

7. Keep warm, dry, and sheltered. Improve shelter if needed.

8. Monitor temperature. And watch for signs and symptoms that will require treatment for Shock (p. 256) or CPR (p. 247).

9. Healing will take time.

Severe hypothermia will require a rapid stabilization of temperature and protection from any further heat loss. Immediate care is needed. The rewarming process is dangerous and can potentially cause heart complications and hypothermic shock.

BITES/STING TREATMENT

Always get the person safely away from whatever caused the bite before treatment.

1. ***Snake Bite***

    A. Remove any jewelry or restrictive clothing near the bite location.

    B. Keep the person calm and breathing in a relaxed state to slow the spread of venom.

    C. Position the bitten area below heart level and restrict movement.

    D. If you have a snake bite kit, use as instructed.

    E. Wrap a bitten limb with a cloth above and below the bite.

    F. Bandage the wound site.

    G. Apply pressure with cold or an ice pack if available.

    H. Monitor for signs and symptoms that would require treatment for Shock (p. 256) or CPR (p. 247).

    I. Seek medical aid if possible.

2. ***Mammal/Reptile/Bird/Fish Bites***

    A. Thoroughly wash the wound with soap and fresh water. Flush mammal bites for at least five minutes.

    B. Treat bleeding and bandage the wound.

    C. Splint or immobilize if needed.

D. Monitor for signs and symptoms that would require treatment for Shock (p. 256) or CPR (p. 247).

E. Seek medical aid if possible.

3. ***Spider Bites and Ant/Scorpion Stings***

A. Keep the person calm and try to relax their breathing.

B. Wash the bite with soap and fresh water.

C. If dangerous venom is suspected, treat as snake bite.

D. Apply pressure with cold or an ice pack if available.

E. Bandage to keep clean.

F. Monitor for allergic reaction at the bite region and especially the person's airway.

G. Seek medical aid if possible.

4. ***Bee/Wasp/Hornet Stings***

A. If a stinger is present, do not squeeze or pinch to remove it because more venom will be released. Scrape across with a credit card or knife edge to get it out.

B. Ask the person if they have a bee sting allergy and if they have an allergy kit.

C. Wash the sting with soap and fresh water.

D. Apply pressure with cold or ice pack if available.

E. Monitor for allergic reaction near the sting and especially the person's airway.

F. Watch for signs and symptoms of anaphylactic shock or any that would require CPR (p. 247).

G. Seek medical aid if possible.

5. ***Stingray/Spiny Fish/Cone Snail/Urchin***

A. Keep the person calm and breathing at a relaxed state to slow the spread of venom.

B. Apply a pressure wrap above the wound to restrict the spread of venom.

C. Soak the wound in hot water for 60-90 minutes.

D. Pain can be severe. Treat as needed.

E. Monitor for signs and symptoms that would require treatment for Shock (p. 256) or CPR (p. 247).

F. Clean the wound with soap and fresh water.

G. Remove any spines or barbs if possible. Deep spines may need surgical removal.

H. Bandage to keep clean.

I. Seek medical aid if possible.

6. ***Jellyfish/Anemones***

A. Gently wash the area with warm seawater. Do not rub.

B. Carefully remove any tentacles by scraping with a credit card or knife edge or by pulling them off with a towel or shirt.

C. Stinging cells can be deactivated by applying vinegar, talcum powder, baking soda, meat tenderizer, or shaving cream but this does not work for all species.

D. Soak the affected area in hot water or apply cold packs.

E. Watch for signs and symptoms that would require treatment for Shock (p. 256) or CPR (p. 247).

F. Seek medical aid if possible.

Always get examined by a medical expert after dangerous bites and stings.

DIRT TIME

Knowing and being prepared to provide care for these types of injuries will bring you above and beyond the average person. You never know when you might need to bind a wound or provide lifesaving care, but you can be equipped to deal with those things when they do happen. Medical supplies and knowledge are very essential to survival. Take the time to build this area into a strong asset.

Work on putting together an ample amount of medical supplies and shore up any gaps in your list. Make sure that you have placed supplies into your vehicles and emergency packs. Be familiar with the inventories and learn how properly to use what you have. Also, think about different items that you would be able to improvise in emergency medical scenarios.

Learn about the things that can cause medical hazards in your area and prepare specifically for those things. It may be poisonous snakes, cold weather, or car accidents. Learn more about these hazards, what you can do to prevent them and the kinds of things you need to treat them.

Take medical courses to build your confidence and level of capability. Classes to learn about CPR and First Aid are held in almost every city. Employers often require many personnel to have training in these areas and they may provide a class or pay for you to take one. The extra ambition might even get you a nod from the boss.

I would also recommend finding a comprehensive medical guide that covers a broad spectrum of different ailments and how to treat them. Learning about the many ways to use local plants for treatments and remedies will also be incredibly helpful. Often, the very things that you need to aid healing are growing close by.

Most of these skills are not extraordinarily complex to master but the difference that they can make could be very impactful.

NOW IT'S UP TO YOU

"WHATEVER THE MIND OF MAN CAN CONCEIVE AND
BELIEVE, IT CAN ACHIEVE."

—NAPOLEON HILL

I am rather confident in my ability to survive and protect those around me, but I make no claim to be an expert or master in the field. I had a martial arts instructor who said that the moment you start to think that you are getting good, prepare to be knocked on your butt. Sure, I may have come up with a few slick ideas along the way, but basically everything that I have learned has been passed to me by another. My skills came from wise elders, from those who took the time to preserve the knowledge in books, from the encouragement and sometimes taunts of friends, from brutal challenges, and from long moments of peaceful observation.

The landscape that encompasses the world of survival is an ever-evolving mixture of nature's laws, trusted old knowledge, and adaptations of the present. In this shifting terrain, there will always be more to learn. Information is plentiful to those who actively seek it. Remember to check the validity of the source but be humble enough to realize that you can learn from unexpected places.

And now you are left with a choice. Granted, the things that you learned from reading will help, but you must expand your abilities with the Dirt Time as well. This is where the skills become something that you can depend upon. Dig into other books and classes that will help you hone specific areas more precisely. Continue challenging yourself to become stronger, more confident and better prepared.

Spread the things that you learn to others who can benefit from it. Growing in these areas will be faster and more dynamic when other minds are involved. We bring stability to ourselves by encouraging strength in the abilities of those around us.

If this book has inspired or positively impacted you in any way, I would like to ask a favor from you. Please share those benefits by giving a copy of Simple Survival to someone you care about. Preventable struggles will persist unless we are able to impact a positive change together. It requires your help.

I know there was a lot covered in the book, but it is merely a solid foundation, the first steps down a long path. It offers a perfect view of the options that you can use to move forward. While some of the next steps will build your aptitude and courage to progress onward, others could lead you to trails that will incite a lifetime of pursuit.

Stay on the path! There is always more ground to cover…

ACKNOWLEDGMENTS

I especially want to thank my family and friends for their support and belief in me. Honor must be given to all of those who have invested precious moments of their lives into my growth and learning. I would also like to give recognition to the readers who help transform a compilation of thoughts and ideas into a stability-based mindset.

As a special thanks, I would like to give credit to all of the people who contributed to the effort that made this book possible. I couldn't have done it without you!

COACHING, SUPPORT AND GUIDANCE:
Self Publishing School

PROFESSIONAL CONSULTATION:
Amanda Van Haren

PROOFREADING:
Peggy Graverson

EDITING:
Qat Wanders, Wandering Words Media

INTERIOR ARTWORK:
Bill Wittmann and Līna Stiprā

COVER ART:
haley_graphics2

INTERIOR LAYOUT:
Melinda Martin, Martin Publishing Services

SELF-PUBLISHING
SCHOOL

NOW IT'S YOUR TURN

Discover the EXACT 3-step blueprint you need to become a bestselling author in 3 months.

Self-Publishing School helped me, and now I want them to help you with this FREE WEBINAR!

Even if you're busy, bad at writing, or don't know where to start, you CAN write a bestseller and build your best life.

With tools and experience across a variety niches and professions, Self-Publishing School is the only resource you need to take your book to the finish line!

DON'T WAIT

Use this link to watch a FREE WEBINAR now, and

Say "YES" to becoming a bestseller:

https://xe172.isrefer.com/go/affegwebinar/bookbrosinc3467

ABOUT THE AUTHOR

J.W. Meyer has devoted a lifetime to the continuous study of survival training. He has spent time serving as a U.S Army Airborne Ranger and later, coaching in leadership and personal development. He is an outdoor adventure enthusiast, world traveler, and advocate for the preservation of nature. His deep admiration for the wilderness has cultivated a spirit that strives to blend with the environment and adapt to its challenges. He currently resides in Europe with his loving wife and two amazing children.

Printed in Great Britain
by Amazon

38935420R00169